T0163352

Catfish, Fiddles, Mules, and More

PROJECT SPONSORS

The Missouri Center for the Book
Western Historical Manuscript Collection, University of
    Missouri–Columbia

SPECIAL THANKS

Lawrence O. Christensen, University of Missouri–Rolla
Gerald Cohen, University of Missouri–Rolla
Laura R. Jolley, Missouri State Archives
Christine Montgomery, State Historical Society of Missouri,
    Columbia
Claudia Powell, Western Historical Manuscript Collection,
    University of Missouri–Columbia
James E. Rathert, Missouri Department of Conservation

MISSOURI HERITAGE READERS
General Editor, Rebecca B. Schroeder

Each Missouri Heritage Reader explores a particular aspect of the state's rich cultural heritage. Focusing on people, places, historical events, and the details of daily life, these books illustrate the ways in which people from all parts of the world contributed to the development of the state and the region. The books incorporate documentary and oral history, folklore, and informal literature in a way that makes these resources accessible to all Missourians.

Intended primarily for adult new readers, these books will also be invaluable to readers of all ages interested in the cultural and social history of Missouri.

BOOKS IN THE SERIES

Catfish, Fiddles, Mules, and More

Missouri's State Symbols

John C. Fisher

University of Missouri Press
Columbia and London

Library of Congress Cataloging-in-Publication Data

Fisher, John C., 1949–
  Catfish, fiddles, mules, and more : Missouri's state symbols /
John C. Fisher.
      p. cm.   (Missouri heritage readers)
Includes bibliographical references (p.) and index.
  ISBN 0-8262-1489-4 (alk. paper)
  1. Emblems, State—Missouri. I. Title. II. Series.
  CR203.T36F57 2003
  929.9—dc22
                                                2003016627

∞™ This paper meets the requirements of the
American National Standard for Permanence of Paper
for Printed Library Materials, Z39.48, 1984.

Designer: Stephanie Foley
Typesetter: Foley Design
Printer and binder: Thomson-Shore, Inc.
Typeface: ITC Korinna

To Carol

Contents

Acknowledgments

While writers spend many hours working alone, no work is a truly solo effort. I wish to express my thanks to all who have participated in this project in any way. In particular, I want to thank Rebecca Schroeder for help in securing photographs and for many valuable suggestions. I also want to express appreciation to the staffs of the State Historical Society of Missouri, the Missouri State Archives, the Department of Conservation, and to Cheryl Seeger of the Division of Geology and Land Survey. They have provided photographs as well as copies of documents and other materials and answered questions.

A special thank-you goes to my friend and fellow writer Rob Simbeck for suggesting this topic to me and also for reading the manuscript and showing me how it could be improved. Finally, I would like to express deep appreciation and thanks to my wife, Carol, for her assistance and encouragement throughout this process. She tirelessly read, corrected, and reread numerous drafts and provided countless ideas for improvement of the manuscript.

Catfish, Fiddles, Mules, and More

Introduction

Mankind has long used symbols of one sort or another. Early hunters made simple drawings on the walls of caves, depicting the animals they sought for food and clothing. Native Americans wore feathers, claws, and teeth, all of which had symbolic meaning to the wearers. Flags have been used to rally armies. The Middle Ages saw the development of coats of arms. All religions employ symbols.

Throughout history, we have used symbols for a variety of reasons. First, they represent values and characteristics. Native Americans adorned themselves with such items as eagles' feathers and bears' claws because the animals had characteristics they admired and hoped to exhibit themselves. Second, symbols convey importance, rank, and authority. In ancient times, kings would seal letters with wax. The king's seal, pressed into the wax while it was soft, made the letter official. The recipient could be sure the letter was authentic. A third reason for using symbols has been to send coded messages. For example, during the early Christian era, when Christians were widely persecuted, revealing one's faith to a stranger could be very dangerous. Thus, a drawing of a fish became a symbol used by Christians to communicate their faith to one another. Non-Christians would not understand the meaning of this symbol. Nations still use seals and flags in much the same way that they have throughout history. Today, states adopt symbols that in some way represent a particular area of the state or something of economic importance to that state.

Missouri has adopted fifteen items to serve as symbols of the state. These range from a song, a folk dance, and a musical instrument through a variety of plants and animals to a mineral, rock, and fossil. All have contributed in some way to the state's history and economy or otherwise helped to identify Missouri as a special place. In addition, Missouri is represented by its great seal, flag, capitol building, a designated Missouri Day, and a widely known nickname.

Researching these symbols has given me a greater appreciation of the state's heritage and the diversity of its land and natural resources. I hope that exploring its symbols in the chapters that follow will provide the reader a similar experience.

1

State Seal

For centuries, kings, noble families, and governments have used seals on official documents. An official seal gave the courier of a document some authority. No one would impede his passage, because to do so would be to challenge the king or other official whose seal was impressed on the parcel he carried. These early seals were usually engraved on wood or metal, and often they were worn as rings.

Missouri's state seal had an active and colorful history from its adoption in 1822 until 1861. It took strong urging from Missouri's first governor, Alexander McNair, to get the general assembly to adopt a design for the seal. Twenty-five years passed before most Missourians knew who had designed it. The original seal was destroyed by fire, and later engravings underwent several obvious changes in appearance, none of which were mandated by law. The seal was even taken out of the state during the Civil War when Missouri, in effect, had two governments. Since that time, life has been calmer for the seal, and it has routinely been used to authenticate official documents.

In 1812, Congress made Missouri a territory of the United States, and six years later the territory petitioned Congress for statehood. Pro- and anti-slavery factions battled to determine whether Missouri would be admitted as a slave or free state. The Missouri Compromise resolved the question in 1820: Maine entered the Union as a free state and Missouri entered as a slave state. On August 10, 1821, Missouri became the

An early engraving of the state seal. (From *Map of the State of Missouri and Illinois from Recent Surveys in the Office of the Surveyor General, St. Louis,* by E. Browne; State Historical Society of Missouri, Columbia)

twenty-fourth state. At that time, Missouri was the western frontier of the United States with fur trading as its biggest industry, though mining and agriculture were also well established in some areas.

Sensitive to the fact that the new state would need a seal to authenticate the acts of its government, Missouri's political leaders provided for an official seal in the state's first constitution, approved in 1820. Section 22 of article 4 stated: "The Secretary of State shall, as soon as may be, procure a seal of state with such emblems and devices as shall be directed by law, which shall not be subject to change." The secretary of state was named as custodian of the seal and has been assigned that role in each constitution since then. The 1820 constitution also provided for the governor to use his personal seal until an official seal could be made available.

Even though the constitution authorized the state's law-makers to produce a seal, they seemed in no hurry to take care of this obligation. Governor McNair, annoyed at not having a state seal, sternly addressed members of the first general assembly, who were meeting at St. Charles, November 6, 1821. "Considerable inconvenience daily arises from the want of a seal of state, and I deem it proper to remind you of the necessity of supplying the deficiency at the present session." In response, a special committee, consisting of Chancey Smith of St. Charles County, James Alcorn of Howard County, and Elias Elston also of Howard County, was appointed to come up with a design.

The following January, the special committee reported back with a bill containing a description of the proposed state seal.

Be it enacted by the General Assembly of the State of Missouri, that the device for an armorial achievement for the state of Missouri, shall be as follows, to wit: Arms, parted per pale, on the dexter side; gules, the white or grisly bear of Missouri, passant guardant, proper on a chief engrailed; azure, a crescent argent; on the sinister side argent, the arms of the United States, the whole with in a band inscribed with the words, "United we stand, divided we fall." For the crest, over the helmet full faced, grated with six bars, or a cloud proper, from which ascends a star argent, and above it a constellation of twenty-three smaller stars argent, on an azure field surrounded by a cloud proper. Supporters on each side, a white or grisly bear of Missouri, rampant, guardant proper, standing on a scroll, inscribed with the motto, "*Salus populi Suprema lex esto,*" and under the scroll the numerical letters MDCCCXX. And the great seal of this state shall be so engraved as to present by its impression, the device of the armorial achievement aforesaid, surrounded by a scroll inscribed with the words, 'the great seal of the state of Missouri' in roman capitals, which seal shall be in a circular form and not more than two and a half inches in diameter.

The bill was approved and signed by Governor McNair on January 11, 1822.

The terms used to describe the state seal appear somewhat strange to us. This is because they are terms of heraldry used to describe coats of arms adopted by families and clans in Europe. These emblems became especially popular during the Middle Ages to distinguish warriors in battle. By the fifteenth century, a formal system had evolved for cataloging and describing arms. A definition of terms helps modern readers to understand the description of the seal:

Arms: figures and colors displayed on shields, banners, etc.
Pale: a broad perpendicular stripe in a coat of arms, centered and occupying one-third of it
Dexter: right (left as you face the shield)
Sinister: left (right as you face the shield)
Gules: red, represented on printed shields by straight perpendicular lines closely drawn together
Passant: walking, applied to any animal on a shield that appears to be walking
Guardant: the face turned toward the viewer
Proper: shown in its natural color
Chief: the upper one-third of the coat of arms
Engrailed: to indent with curved lines as a line of division
Azure: blue
Crescent: the shape of a new moon
Argent: silver
Crest: an addition to the shield, placed over it, usually on a wreath
Or: gold
Rampant: an animal standing upright on the hind legs

Thus, Missouri's state seal was designed according to the system used to describe heraldic emblems.

The committee chose emblems that represented something about the state. They chose the grizzly bear because of

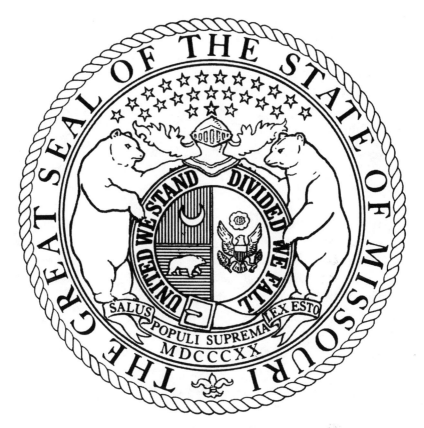

The state seal engraving currently in use. (State Historical Society of Missouri, Columbia)

its great size and strength and because they believed it was unique to the Missouri River and its tributaries. The crescent moon indicated that the state was beginning and increasing in size and importance. This type of moon was used in heraldry only by a second son, indicating that Missouri was the second state formed out of the Louisiana Purchase. The arms of the United States and of the state, encircled by a band but separated by a pale, or perpendicular line, indicated that the whole makes one government, yet the state and United

States government are separate and distinct governments for some purposes. The helmet indicates sovereignty of the state. The large star at the top represents Missouri rising to become a part of the union. The translation of the Latin motto is: "Let the welfare of the people be the supreme law."

Once the general assembly passed the bill and it was signed by the governor, legislators must have thought that the story of Missouri's state seal would be complete. However, that was not the case. First of all, no official record exists of who actually designed the seal. Neither the house nor the senate journal of the time identify the designer, although historians now believe it was Robert Williams Wells. This is based on a letter Wells wrote in 1847 that was published in the *Jefferson City Metropolitan*. He was writing in response to an address by Edward Bates on February 17, 1847, at a celebration of the founding of St. Louis. Bates incorrectly interpreted the motto on the seal, *"Salus popui suprema lex esto."* Wells wrote to correct Bates's error, as well as to give an interpretation of the other elements. In this letter, Wells states that he is "the author or the original suggestor of our coat of arms."

In the intervening years, Wells's letter seems to have been forgotten, and controversy continued about who designed the original seal. His letter was eventually discovered by Roy T. King, who published an article about Wells in the January 1936 issue of the *Missouri Historical Review*. King's article discusses others also credited with designing the seal.

In Howard County, people had long believed that George F. Burckhartt was the designer; however, there was no written record to support that tradition, which rested primarily on the testimony of descendants and relatives of Burckhartt. Louis Houck, author of *History of Missouri,* speculated that Nathaniel Beverly Tucker was the designer. King concluded that the case was strongest for Wells: First of all, he was the only person to publicly state that he was the author. Second, his letter was the earliest publication making a claim of authorship, coming only twenty-five years after adoption of

The state seal used by the secretary of state's office to authenticate official documents. (Townsend Godsey Foundation, State Historical Society of Missouri, Columbia)

the seal. Third, there is no record that anyone disputed Wells's claim. Both Burckhartt and Tucker were still living at the time Wells wrote the letter as were others involved with the seal's adoption. Wells also had served in the Missouri General Assembly, as attorney general, and as a United States district judge.

Over the years, the seal's appearance has changed. The law enacted in 1822, which established the design of the state seal, was rather specific about what its appearance should be. The constitution states that it is not to be changed. However, each new engraving of the seal incorporated several changes for no apparent reason and certainly not by mandate of law.

According to the state treasurer's journal, on March 27, 1822, Otis Peck was paid $160.00 for engraving the seal. The appearance of this seal conforms to its description in the law, and this engraving remained in use until 1837. On November 15 of that year, fire destroyed the state's capitol. Much was lost, including the original engraving of the state seal. A second engraving followed. Indirect evidence suggests that this one was made by Robert L. Campbell of St. Louis. The engraving on this seal was not of very high quality; it may have been completed in haste since there was urgent need for a replacement, and some obvious changes were made in the design. The supporting bears are turned three-quarter view instead of facing outward. The band around the arms is a belt with the buckle at the bottom. The eagle's head on the United States emblem is turned to the right instead of to the left. Finally, the crescent moon is turned perpendicular instead of horizontal with the cusps pointing upward.

On February 29, 1840, the state began using a third engraving of the seal. There appears to have been no reason for making this engraving unless it was to correct the errors in the 1838 seal. Made by Edward Stabler, it is of much higher quality than the previous one. The Stabler engraving retains the belt buckle and three-quarter view of the bears, but the eagle is turned correctly as is the crescent moon. This was the seal in use in 1861, which Governor Claiborne F. Jackson removed from the capitol on June 12, when he was forced out of Jefferson City by Union troops. Jackson's administration continued to function with the deposed general assembly meeting in Neosho, where it formally withdrew from the Union and joined the Confederacy. When Jackson died in 1862, Lieutenant Governor Thomas C. Reynolds took over the exiled government, which eventually made its headquarters in Marshall, Texas. The government-in-exile had possession of the Stabler seal until the end of the war. Reynolds did not return it to the state until 1869.

To replace the seal taken by Missouri's Confederate government, Thomas Haynes of St. Louis engraved a new seal. The differences in the Haynes seal are a major change to the appearance of the helmet above the arms and a slight difference in the appearance of the bears. According to the secretary of state's office, this seal has been the standard for all subsequent engravings, which show only very minor variations. It is interesting to note the evolution of the supporting bears in the seal from fuzzy, youthful animals to more sleek, robust, mature creatures.

There have been numerous artist drawings of the seal for use by state agencies on letterheads and envelopes. These have varied in appearance. The seal has also been incorporated into decorative sculpture at the east entry of the capitol building. Today, as provided in the state constitution, the secretary of state is custodian of the seal. That office impresses it on all official documents signed by the governor and attested to by the secretary of state.

2

State Flag

Flags as symbols have led armies into battle, claimed new territories, and given identity to groups and places. Military units have used flags to keep their troops together and to prevent attack by their own members. Flags have the power to bring out strong emotional responses. Despite flags' importance for identification and their prominence throughout history, Missourians did not seem to be in any hurry to select a state flag. It was not until ninety-two years after statehood that Missouri selected an official flag. On March 22, 1913, Governor Elliot Major signed a law giving Missouri its first and only official flag.

Even though Missouri did not adopt an official flag until 1913, other banners had flown over the area before and after statehood. Missouri was one of the states carved out of the Louisiana Territory. France and Spain swapped control of this region twice between 1762 and 1803. The first flag in what is now Missouri was the French *fleur de lis,* the banner carried by early French explorers who claimed the vast area of Louisiana for France. France transferred control of the territory to Spain in 1762, near the end of the Seven Years' War in Europe. The Spanish Cross of Burgundy flag, a red St. Andrews cross on a white field, was the next flag to fly over Louisiana. In 1785, Spain changed its flag to one with red and gold horizontal stripes. The Treaty of 1796 returned the region to French control in 1800. At this time, the French flag had red, white, and blue vertical stripes. The United States

Marie Elizabeth Oliver was the designer of Missouri's flag.
(Missouri State Archives)

purchased Louisiana from France for fifteen million dollars in 1803, making the stars and stripes the fifth flag to fly over Missouri.

Missouri's territorial period and the early years of statehood saw no consideration given to a state flag. During the Civil War, several flags representing various Missouri Confederate military units appeared. The *Ste. Genevieve Plaindealer* reported in March 1861 that a flag consisting of a blue field with the state coat of arms in gold in the center was raised over the St. Louis courthouse, reportedly placed there by St. Louis Minutemen, a military group sympathetic to the South. The flag was removed by county officials. A short time later, according to the *Plaindealer,* the Minutemen hoisted a second flag at their headquarters. This flag consisted of a blue field, a crescent, a cross, and a single star. This drew crowds of both Union and Confederate sympathizers, and threats were made by each side, but the tension eased for a time. The growing Confederate sympathy led to formation of the Missouri State Guard in 1861 as a defense against federal invasion forces in Missouri. The State Guard used a flag with a blue field and the state emblem in gold. Other Confederate units from Missouri also had their own flags.

The formation of the pro-Union Home Guard in St. Louis in early 1861, Captain Nathaniel Lyon's controversial seizure of Camp Jackson on May 10, 1861, and the failure of Governor Jackson's attempt to keep Missouri neutral soon brought the Civil War to the state. After the war, no attention was given to the lack of a state flag until 1908. The Missouri Daughters of the American Revolution (DAR), meeting in Columbia, discussed whether Missouri had a state flag. Mrs. Samuel Green, state regent, appointed a committee of five to investigate the question and to prepare a design if Missouri did not have a flag. The state history of the DAR indicates that the committee never met, but Marie Elizabeth Watkins Oliver of Cape Girardeau, a member of that committee, took it upon herself to research the issue. She found that Missouri did not have a

The state flag. (Missouri State Archives)

flag. She then contacted the secretary of state in every state asking for and receiving copies of the designs of their flags and the laws establishing them.

Following her research, Oliver enlisted the assistance of Mary Kochtitzky, an artist from Cape Girardeau, to prepare a painting of Oliver's design. Robert Burett Oliver, Marie Oliver's husband and a former state senator, prepared a draft of a bill to introduce his wife's design as the state flag. His nephew, Arthur L. Oliver, state senator from Pemiscot County, introduced the bill March 17, 1909, in the Missouri State Senate. The flag design described in this bill had three horizontal stripes of red, white, and blue. In the center was the state seal surrounded by a blue band with twenty-four five-pointed stars. The bill won approval in the senate in April, but it was defeated in the house.

On February 4, 1909, G. H. Holcomb, a state representative from Jackson County, introduced a bill in the house containing a different design for a state flag. The Holcomb design called for thirteen stripes of alternating red and white. The upper left corner was to be blue and imprinted with "MO" in Gothic style. The Holcomb bill was also defeated in the house. Critics of the Holcomb design felt that it resembled the flag of the United States too closely and that it did nothing to symbolize Missouri.

In 1911, the Oliver design was again introduced in the senate, where it won approval for a second time. Unfortunately, the state capitol burned February 5, destroying the original painting of the flag. For this reason, the design was never brought to a vote in the house. Representative Holcomb brought his design to the house for a second time in January 1911. It won approval there in March but failed in the senate.

Oliver set about making a second image of her design of the flag, this one of silk. Mrs. S. D. MacFarland, a former St. Louis resident who lived in Pasadena, California, painted the state seal on the flag. This flag was sent to Jefferson City to be viewed by members of the general assembly. The Missouri Daughters of the American Revolution and the Colonial Dames of Missouri both gave their support to the Oliver design and urged state legislators to approve that design.

Charles C. Oliver, representative from Cape Girardeau County, introduced the Oliver flag bill in the house on January 21, 1913. It was approved March 7 and sent to the senate. There, it was approved for the third time. Governor Elliott W. Major then signed the bill on March 22. At last Missouri had its own official flag.

Missouri has never adopted an official pledge of allegiance to its flag. In 1979, Representative Howard Christian introduced House Bill 780, which contained wording for a pledge. Referred to committee, it apparently received no further action. The pledge, contained in that bill, written by David W. Short, reads as follows:

I pledge allegiance to the flag
Of the sovereign State of Missouri
And the honor it contains.
One State, a United State of America,
Under God,
Shall let the welfare of the people
Be the supreme law.

Various organizations within the state have developed their own pledges and salutes to the Missouri flag. Here are two examples:

Missouri Daughters of the American Revolution
I pledge allegiance to the flag of Missouri and to the ideals for which it stands. United with other states for the benefit of all, we march forward to a greater America.

Missouri United Daughters of the Confederacy
I salute the Missouri State Flag and the principles for which it stands. May the good of the people always be supreme law.

3

Capitol Building

Locating and preserving their seat of government has been a problem for Missourians. There have been three capital cities and six capitol buildings (more if the exiled government during the Civil War is counted).

Leaders held the state's first constitutional convention at the Mansion Hotel in St. Louis, and the first general assembly met at the Missouri Hotel, also in St. Louis. Because of its prominence in trade when Missouri gained statehood, St. Louis would seem to have had an advantage in the selection process for a capital location. However, the general assembly selected St. Charles as the temporary location for the state capital. From 1821 until 1826, the state government operated out of rooms in three adjoining buildings. The general location of the permanent capital was designated in Article 10 of the constitution. It provided that it should be on the Missouri River within forty miles of the mouth of the Osage River. On December 31, 1821, the general assembly approved the site of present-day Jefferson City as the capital.

The first government building, completed in 1826, was both a meeting place for the general assembly and living quarters for the governor. In 1833, a governor's residence was built near the capitol. Fire destroyed the capitol in 1837. While the new building was under construction, the state used the Cole County courthouse for official business. The second Jefferson City capitol was finished in 1840. The new governor's mansion was not built until 1871.

Ceres, goddess of agriculture, atop the capitol dome in Jefferson City. (Missouri Department of Agriculture)

In 1861, federal troops forced Governor Claiborne Jackson and much of the general assembly out of Jefferson City. They met at the Masonic hall in Neosho to formally withdraw Missouri from the Union. After Jackson's death in 1862, Lieutenant Governor Thomas C. Reynolds assumed leadership of the exiled government and established a seat of government first in Little Rock, Arkansas, then in Shreveport, Louisiana, and finally in Marshall, Texas. Thus, Missouri has the distinction of having had capitals located outside the state.

The capitol completed in 1840 served as the seat of Missouri's government until 1911, undergoing two years of major remodeling beginning in 1887. This renovation was completed in 1889. On February 5, 1911, lightning struck the dome and caused a fire that destroyed the building.

Missouri now had to build its third capitol in Jefferson City. The general assembly created the State Capitol Commission Board on March 24, 1911, and proposed a $3.5 million bond issue. A special election was held in August, and the measure was approved. The board visited the capitols of a number of states and sought competitive architectural drawings with the cooperation of the American Institute of Architects. An advisory group of three architects recommended the design of New York architects Evarts Tracy and Egerton Swartwout. Their plan won acceptance, and ground-breaking ceremonies were held May 6, 1913. In November 1913, a contract was awarded to John Gill and Sons of Cleveland, Ohio, who completed the structure in 1917 at a cost of $4,215,000, which included furnishings.

Missouri's present capitol, constructed of native limestone quarried near Carthage, is an impressive building situated on the bluffs along the Missouri River. Its dome rises 238 feet above the ground. A bronze statue of the goddess Ceres, the Roman goddess of agriculture, stands atop the dome. The capitol has eight 48-foot columns on the south side and six 40-foot columns on the north. It also has two bronze doors, each measuring 13 feet by 18 feet. The five-story building is

Many Missouri schoolchildren visit the state capitol each spring.
(Missouri State Archives)

437 feet long, 300 feet wide in the center, 200 feet wide in the
wings, and contains 500,000 square feet of floor space.

The fund established to build the capitol produced more
money than was needed for construction. This allowed the
funding of outstanding artwork that complemented the building and grounds. The artists whose works decorate the capitol building and grounds included some of the best in the
United States. One distinctive feature on the grounds is a
large bronze sculpture by Karl Bitters, depicting the signing
of the Louisiana Purchase. Murals cover several of the capitol's interior walls. Particularly noteworthy are those in the
senate lounge by Missouri artist Thomas Hart Benton. With
the murals, the artist created controversy over the way he
chose to depict Missouri history. Benton did not fill the murals
with the faces of famous Missourians, but rather sought to

trace the state's social history through the images of "ordinary" Missourians performing the tasks and activities of daily life. According to Benton, he was not trying to show specific historical events but to show "the social conditions in which they occurred."

The capitol, a major tourist attraction, houses the state senate and house of representatives. There are also offices for the governor, lieutenant governor, secretary of state, treasurer, and state auditor, as well as some administrative offices. The Missouri State Museum is located on the first floor.

4

State Flower

Hawthorn

Shakespeare said, "a rose by any other name would smell as sweet." The state flower isn't the rose, but it is a member of the rose family. The hawthorn, or red haw (*Crataegus spp.*), became Missouri's state flower on March 16, 1923. Like the rose, it has beautiful, showy blossoms and lots of thorns. In a sense, it is a rose by another name.

Marie L. Goodman first suggested a state flower for Missouri at a meeting of the Missouri State Horticultural Society in January 1916. A committee consisting of Goodman, H. C. Irish (president of the society), and H. S. Wayman (secretary) was set up to recommend a flower. They sent a letter asking for nominations for a state flower to society members, the Missouri Federation of Women's Clubs, other organizations across the state, and the press. Each flower nominated had to be beautiful in color and form, native to the state, abundant, and widely distributed over the state. The society reported the survey's results in December 1916. The wild crab apple received the highest number of votes, followed by the wild rose. Aster, honeysuckle, black-eyed Susan, violet, hollyhock, and burdock also received nominations. The Missouri State Horticultural Society endorsed the wild crab apple and drafted legislation for its formal nomination. Ben F. Stuart introduced the measure in the house; however, the bill failed.

The next major effort to secure a state flower came from the Missouri Daughters of the American Revolution. At their

The hawthorn has showy blossoms. (Missouri Department of Conservation, photo by Jim Rathert)

state meeting in 1919, they proposed the daisy. The following day they learned that the daisy is not native to Missouri and that it had already been adopted by North Carolina. The group next endorsed Mrs. Waller Washington Graves's nomination of the hawthorn. At their state meeting the following year, the DAR again endorsed the hawthorn as the state flower. In 1922, the general assembly considered both the hawthorn and daisy. The hawthorn bill was approved by the senate but failed in the house. The DAR immediately started seeking support for a hawthorn bill in the next term. They received many endorsements from state organizations, including the Missouri State Teachers Association, Missouri Sons of the Revolution, and Missouri Federated Women's Clubs. F. B. Mumford, head of the University of Missouri–Columbia Department of Agriculture, and B. R. Coleman, president of the Missouri State Horticultural Society, also gave their support.

Sarah Lucille Turner, a representative from Kansas City and one of two women elected to the Missouri General Assembly in 1922, introduced a bill in 1923 proposing the hawthorn for the state flower. A similar measure was introduced in the senate. Turner's bill passed the house and was then substituted for the original senate bill, winning approval. Governor Arthur M. Hyde signed the bill on March 16, 1923.

Hawthorns are a very large and complex group of plants with well over one hundred species in the United States. Many of these are difficult to distinguish even for botanists. In fact, the state legislature did not choose a species when designating the state flower. It named the entire genus, *Crataegus.* The hawthorn is certainly an appropriate representative of the state. It is found throughout Missouri, growing as shrubs or small trees. The tallest members of the group reach about thirty feet. There are currently four species of hawthorn listed on the Department of Conservation's state champion tree list. A cockspur hawthorn in Carrollton is twenty-one feet tall; a downy hawthorn in Kansas City reaches twenty-eight feet; a fleshy hawthorn in Kirkwood measures eight feet; and a green hawthorn in Butler County is thirty-five feet tall. Hawthorns will adapt to a wide variety of soil conditions. In fact, they will grow in all parts of the state. Their dark, grayish brown bark breaks into scaly plates on older trees. Hawthorn leaves have lobed or toothed edges.

The hawthorn produces gorgeous, large clusters of white flowers, which appear in April and May. The flowers resemble those of the apple, to which the hawthorn is closely related. These blossoms earned the hawthorn its place as a state emblem. The flowers produce red berries, which look like miniature apples. The berries, ripening before frost, provide food for wildlife such as squirrels, raccoons, opossums, quail, wild turkeys, deer, and robins. They were also used by early settlers in Missouri to make jelly. Although the hawthorn is very thorny, the thorns aren't all bad. A variety of songbirds take advantage of the hawthorn as a safe and protected place to build nests. It grows primarily in open areas and is an opportunist that will invade an uncultivated field or unmowed pasture. Cattle will usually avoid it because of its thorns.

The hawthorn is too small to be much used for lumber although it has been used to make shuttles for looms. Both the flowers and berries make it ornamental; however, its susceptibility to a number of diseases and insects limits its usefulness. Fireblight, rust, and leaf spot are among the bacterial and fungal diseases that attack hawthorn. Borers, scales, aphids, spider mites, and other insects can infest the plant. However, a few varieties have been developed that have some resistance to disease. The thorns sometimes limit where hawthorn can be planted as an ornamental. It must be placed so as to minimize contact by animals and people.

The hawthorn has long been used to make an herbal heart tonic in many parts of the world. Preparations made from the fruit and leaves dilate the coronary arteries of the heart and reduce blood pressure with effects similar to those of the commonly prescribed medicine digitalis. Hawthorn use in medicine has been most extensively studied in Germany.

Brightening the spring with showy blossoms and providing food and shelter for wildlife are two of the hawthorn's favorable qualities. Its thorny nature and tendency to invade areas where it hasn't been invited are some of its less desirable characteristics. On balance, however, because of its widespread adaptability within the state and the unsurpassed beauty of its flowers, the hawthorn serves Missouri well as its state floral emblem.

5

State Tree

Flowering Dogwood

Nestled under a canopy of towering oaks, the trees go unnoticed most of the year. However, from mid-April until early May, the wooded areas of the southern two-thirds of Missouri are aglow with the brilliant white blossoms of the flowering dogwood, *Cornus florida*. Even though dogwood is mostly found in the Ozarks, it also appears in several counties north of the Missouri River. This harbinger of spring and summer became Missouri's state tree in 1955 through legislation introduced by Icie Mae Pope of Webster County and Jim Banner of Camden County.

The dogwood grows best as an understory in hardwood forests because of its tolerance of shade. Dogwoods prefer moist, well-drained soil. Being shallow-rooted, they are intolerant of drought. Rarely, they can reach a maximum height of forty feet with a branch spread of thirty-five feet. Flowers appear before any leaves are on the plant. The actual flowers on the dogwood, small yellowish green clusters, are not very showy. They are surrounded, however, by four large bracts, or modified leaves, with notched tips, which resemble petals and give the dogwood blossom its beauty.

The flowering dogwood's foliage, which has a glossy green upper surface and a dull gray-green lower surface, is nearly as attractive as its flowers. Leaves turn purplish to scarlet in the fall, adding beauty to yet another season. Even the bark of the flowering dogwood is distinctive. Brownish and rough

The flowering dogwood grows as an understory tree in hardwood forests. (Missouri Department of Conservation, photo by Jim Rathert)

and broken into small square plates, it stands out in the winter landscape.

Dogwood flowers produce small egg-shaped fruit measuring about one-half inch in length. This fruit turns from bright green to a reddish color by autumn and provides food for many types of wildlife, including several species of birds as well as chipmunks, squirrels, deer, and others. Rabbits and deer eat the bark, twigs, and leaves in winter. Because of the openness of its branches, birds do not often use the tree for nesting.

The dogwood has also become a widely planted ornamental in urban areas. Because of its limited size and its attractiveness in all seasons it is well suited to many locations and landscaping plans. Under good conditions, it grows quite rapidly the first few years after planting, then growth slows. The flowering dogwood benefits from being planted where it will

Dogwood blossoms signal spring's arrival. (Missouri Department of Conservation, photo by Jim Rathert)

receive partial shade. Although the native flowering dogwood has predominately white flowers, a few trees bear pink blossoms. There are also several cultivated varieties that have red or pink blossoms.

While the dogwood is not considered to be of commercial importance for lumber now, the wood has had some unusual uses over the years. Its close-grained nature and high shock resistance has made it suitable for golf club heads, mallet heads, handles for chisels, wedges, pulleys, spindles, jeweler's blocks, knitting needles, and shuttles for looms. It is well adapted for rough uses because it wears smoothly and evenly.

One has to wonder how such a beautiful tree came to have such a common name. Two quite different stories attempt to explain the origins of the name. In its book *Missouri Trees*, the Missouri Conservation Department relates a story tying the name to the word *dag,* meaning dagger or skewer. Butchers used "dagwood" to make skewers. In time, the name was changed to dogwood. Another explanation connects the name to a practice by dog owners in Europe, who sometimes boiled the bark of the European species in water and used the resulting mixture to treat mange.

The dogwood's showy blossoms have inspired numerous poems and several legends. There are legends associated with Greek mythology and with Cherokee Indian lore. In fact, the variety of dogwood with red blooms is named Cherokee. Probably the most widely known legend is the one that associates the wood of the dogwood with the cross on which Jesus was crucified. The tree, the legend goes, was sorrowful for being used in this way. In pity, Christ promised that the dogwood would never again grow large enough to be used to make a cross. Each flower would be in the form of a cross with a rust-colored notch at the end of each bract, signifying the nails used to hold Jesus on the cross.

While Missouri doesn't have the national champion dogwood tree—trees in North Carolina and Virginia are currently tied for that honor—it does host some noteworthy specimens. The flowering dogwood tree with the largest trunk, measuring seventy-nine inches in circumference, is located in Jackson, in Cape Girardeau County, on the property of John Knaup. The dogwood sporting the greatest height (thirty-four feet) and the greatest spread (forty-nine feet) is on Margaret Thurmond's property in Charleston, located in Mississippi County.

When the general assembly enacted the statute naming the flowering dogwood as the state tree, it also directed the state department of agriculture to encourage its cultivation. As a result, the dogwood now grows statewide as a landscape tree, except in the extreme northern counties. During the early spring, just about anywhere in the state people can enjoy the dogwood's radiant blossoms. They serve as a reminder that the season of rebirth is beginning.

6

State Tree Nut

Black Walnut

The black walnut was a symbol of Missouri even before it was adopted officially on July 9, 1990. The production of top-grade walnut lumber and delicious nuts has been synonymous with this state for many years. Because it provides both lumber and a food product, the walnut is unquestionably the most valuable tree in Missouri.

The black walnut (*Juglans nigra*) is native to the entire eastern half of the United States. There are several other species of walnut trees. The English walnut (*Juglans regia*) is widely grown in California and has a large commercial market, but it is not native to the United States. Another native species is the butternut or white walnut (*Juglans cinerea*). It also grows over much of the eastern United States and produces good-quality lumber, but the nuts are of little commercial value.

The black walnut is a large tree; some trees reach heights of more than one hundred feet. Walnut leaves are one to two feet long and contain fifteen to twenty-three leaflets that turn yellow in the fall. Both male and female flowers are produced on the same tree. The female flowers develop into globe-shaped fruit with a yellowish-green husk that turns black as the nut matures. Iodine in the husks will stain a handlers' hands brown. Under this husk is a nut with a rough, dark brown to black shell. Ranging from one and one-half to two and one-half inches in diameter, the nut contains an oily meat with a strong, distinctive, sweet flavor.

Missouri is the nation's leading producer of black walnuts.
(Missouri Department of Conservation, photo by Jim Rathert)

Walnuts are found growing across the state in a variety of habitats, but the trees prefer a location with deep, well-drained soil, such as river-bottom land that is not regularly flooded. Their tap roots can reach down seven feet or more if no barriers, such as rocks in the soil, stop them. The state champion walnut tree is a specimen growing in Fayette. This giant is 87 feet tall and has a circumference of 207 inches.

Although it grows widely across the state, the walnut tree is plagued by a number of fungal diseases. Anthracnose, leaf spot, and white mold are the most common. In some years, these diseases will cause premature defoliation of entire trees in late summer. Fortunately, unless the diseases become severe, they usually do little permanent harm to the trees. The walnut caterpillar and fall webworm are two insects that also attack walnut trees, although they usually do not cause any long-term damage. Insects and disease will become of greater concern as walnuts are planted more often in orchard settings, where there are large numbers of trees in relatively small areas.

Black walnut lumber is the most valuable lumber produced in the state. It is heavy and strong with a fine grain. Most walnut lumber is used to produce high-quality furniture and gunstocks. Walnut logs, sawed into very thin slices, also provide veneer. These slices are then glued to less expensive woods to make furniture that appears to be made of walnut. Missouri leads the nation in the production of walnut lumber and has done so for many years.

When we think about walnut trees, the wonderfully flavored nuts they produce always come to mind. Here again, Missouri is the leader. Hammons Products Company in Stockton is the top supplier of walnut products in the world. In 2000, it purchased 8.5 million pounds of walnuts. Missouri usually produces 60 to 65 percent of the nation's walnut crop, most of which comes from wild trees. Firms that buy walnuts set up hulling machinery in specific locations. Anyone who has access to walnut trees can pick up the nuts and bring them to hulling locations. Here the outer hull is removed and payment made on the basis of hulled weight. Black walnut nut meats are used in a variety of baked goods, candies, and ice cream. Many traditional Ozark recipes feature the nuts. Black walnuts also provide an abundant food source for wildlife.

Even the nut shells can be used. They are ground to make an abrasive product that is used to clean and polish a wide variety of materials such as plastic, soft metals, fiberglass, wood, and stone. This product works well for cleaning and polishing gun casings, engine parts, electrical parts, and jewelry, and for preparing surfaces for painting anywhere a mild abrasive is needed. Manufacturers use ground walnut shells to make soaps, cosmetics, and dental cleansers, as well as fillers in dynamite and as filtering material. They are often used in oil drilling to prevent the loss of drilling fluids.

Parts of the walnut tree have also served medicinal purposes. Native Americans made a tea from the inner bark to use as a laxative and chewed the bark for toothaches. Today, preparations made from green walnut hulls are sold in herbal markets for a variety of uses, including treatment of skin fungus, ringworm, internal parasites, and constipation.

Walnut roots produce a substance called juglone, which is toxic to some plants. A toxic zone extends fifty to sixty feet from a mature tree, which is a drawback to using black walnut in landscape planting. Plants most sensitive to the substance include apples, azaleas, blackberries, some chrysanthemums, lilacs, peonies, peppers, petunias, and tomatoes. Most grasses are unaffected by juglone. Since juglone is also found in other parts of the walnut tree, its leaves and hulls should not be used in mulch or as compost material.

Because the black walnut is such a valuable tree, researchers encourage its planting in both ornamental and commercial settings. Scientists at the University of Missouri are striving to improve the genetic traits of walnut tree stock to increase the productivity and quality of both lumber and nuts. Others are developing ways landowners can plant walnut trees and grow other crops in between the trees so they can earn income from the land while the trees are maturing.

There could hardly be a more fitting symbol for Missouri than the black walnut. The tree produces more nuts and lumber in Missouri than in any other state while enhancing the beauty of the landscape and providing food for wildlife.

7

State Bird

Bluebird

What displays beautiful flashes of sky blue color, sings a cheery song, and destroys insects by the thousands? The bluebird, of course. There is nothing to dislike about the bluebird. No wonder it was designated the Missouri state bird. It is also one of our older symbols, having been adopted March 30, 1927. New York is the only other state to have the eastern bluebird as its state bird. Michael Kinney of St. Louis introduced the legislation giving the bluebird official status in Missouri. Kinney holds the distinction of having served longer in the state senate than any other member. First elected in 1912, he retired in 1968.

The eastern bluebird (*Sialia sialis*) is a member of the thrush family, which is noted for its singers. The familiar robin also belongs to this family. Bluebirds are six to seven inches long. The male has a blue back and reddish brown throat and breast; the female also has a reddish breast, but she is more grayish on the back with blue primarily in the wings. The backs of immature birds are blue with flecks of white while the breasts are white with dark spots. Young males have more blue than young females. The favorite habitat for bluebirds is rural grasslands that contain scattered trees. This includes pastures, roadsides, power line rights-of-way, and farmlands. Mowed grassy areas, such as golf courses and large lawns, provide suitable habitat as well. In these kinds of areas, bluebirds can easily find their favorite foods—insects such as grasshoppers, crickets, katydids, beetles, and some flying insects. They will also feed on earthworms, spiders, millipedes, centipedes, sow bugs, and snails. During the winter, bluebirds rely heavily on wild berries to sustain them. These include the fruit of dogwood, hawthorn, wild grape, sumac, hackberry, honeysuckle, Virginia creeper, red cedar, and poke.

Because bluebirds favor open grasslands, they benefited when the settlement of North America began. Pioneers converted forests into pastures and orchards, which created more feeding habitat. Bluebirds seek natural cavities in trees for nesting sites. Holes first made by woodpeckers in dead trees are ideal. Woodpeckers and natural decay also produced cavities in wooden fence posts, which provided additional nesting sites, allowing bluebird numbers to increase through the mid-1800s.

Beginning in the late 1800s, several factors led to a dramatic decrease in bluebird numbers. First of all, the European starling and the English house sparrow were introduced to North America. These very aggressive birds are also cavity nesters. They soon took over large numbers of nesting sites that had been used by bluebirds. The replacement of wooden fence posts with those made of steel and the removal of dead and dying trees along field borders and fencerows further reduced nesting sites.

Fortunately, well-planned management programs have helped to increase the bluebird population. The programs use bluebird trails, or lines of nest boxes that bluebirds readily use. Boxes are spaced one hundred yards or more apart in an area with favorable habitat. The boxes must then be monitored to keep competitive species, such as the house sparrow, from occupying them. Specific directions for constructing and locating nest boxes are available from the Missouri Conservation Department.

The eastern bluebird is found over the entire eastern half of North America. It ranges from the southern parts of Newfoundland, Quebec, and Manitoba in Canada south to the

The eastern bluebird.
(Missouri Department
of Conservation, photo
by Jim Rathert)

Gulf Coast. In the United States, it may be found from the East Coast to the foothills of the Rocky Mountains. Bluebirds are common in all of Missouri except the southeast lowlands. They overwinter as far north as mid-Missouri but generally leave areas farther north for warmer climates from September through mid-December. Migrating birds return in February to begin nest site selection. In areas where bluebirds stay through the winter, they will form small flocks and stay close to where berries, used for winter food, are abundant.

Both male and female bluebirds are devoted parents. The male selects a nest site, and the female builds the nest of soft grasses and incubates the eggs. Both parents feed the young, which leave the nest in fifteen to eighteen days. The female then prepares the nest for a second brood. Three to six eggs are laid each time. Occasionally, a pair will produce three broods in a season.

Bluebirds are simply a joy to watch. Thanks to the many individuals and groups who establish and maintain nest boxes, populations of the state bird are secure for future generations to enjoy.

8

State Animal

Mule

When the word *mule* is mentioned, the caricature of a slow, lazy, floppy-eared creature hitched to a plow or wagon often comes to mind. While the mule does have rather long ears and often has been used for pulling plows and wagons, the other attributes hardly describe the animal that became Missouri's state animal in 1995—the Missouri mule.

Many people today may not be fully aware of just what sort of animal a mule is. When a female horse (mare) and a male donkey (jack) are crossed, the resulting offspring is called a mule. The offspring of a cross between a female donkey (jennet or jenny) and a male horse (stallion) is called a hinny. Hinnies are often small and are not as useful as mules. Since mules result from the crossbreeding of two species, they are hybrids and are, therefore, sterile; they do not reproduce. There have been some very rare exceptions, when a female mule has given birth after being mated with a stallion or jack. But in a sense, the mule is really an animal invented by man. Horses and donkeys in the wild rarely, if ever, interbreed.

Mules have a long history of working for man. They are mentioned a number of times in the Old Testament. A mule-drawn carriage transported Alexander the Great's coffin, and Romans used mules in their conquests. Spain became a leader in mule breeding after being conquered by the Moors in the eighth century. In the tenth century, mule breeding in France began to develop. The mule was slower to gain

Guy Griffin and "Missy," four-time first-place winner at the Missouri State Fair. (*St. Joseph News-Press*, photo by Ival Lawhon, Jr.)

acceptance in Great Britain; however, the British government purchased many for use by the military and for transportation in its colonies, especially India. Mule use in the New World began as soon as Europeans started its exploration.

Mules make excellent work animals. According to Melvin Bradley, writing in *The Missouri Mule: His Origin and Times*, they are highly intelligent and can be taught a work skill in about half the time it takes to teach a horse. Bradley also states that mules are strong-willed, but not stubborn. They seem to have an instinct for self-preservation that makes them resist placing themselves in dangerous situations.

Mules are more surefooted than horses and are regularly used to carry people and supplies along steep rocky trails, such as those that lead to the floor of the Grand Canyon. When kept in large groups in feedlots, mules are less prone to fighting and suffer fewer injuries than horses kept under the same conditions. They can also be fed grain and hay free-choice, whereas horses fed in the same way will founder. Well-trained mules also tend to be less excitable in crowds than horses. They are somewhat longer-lived than horses and also less susceptible to disease. Because they can survive hard conditions and a poor food supply, mules maintain their strength and stay in better condition than horses when hauling freight long distances.

George Washington deserves much credit for starting the mule-breeding industry in the United States. He felt that large, strong mules would be far superior to horses for use in agriculture. However, in the late 1700s, such mules simply didn't exist in this country. Washington managed to get embargoes lifted, which allowed the importation of jack and jennet stock from Spain and France. Washington's efforts attracted the attention of other breeders, and soon large numbers of jacks and jennets were being imported. Breeding efforts spread westward into Kentucky and Tennessee. By the 1800s, breeders had been able to blend characteristics from these various sources into a new, large breed called the American Mammoth Jack. Jacks of this type, when crossed with draft mares, produced the large, strong mules so much in demand. This type of jack later contributed to Missouri's mule industry and led to the development of the "Missouri mule."

The opening of the Santa Fe Trail in 1821 gave a boost to Missouri's mule-breeding industry. The trail, running between Franklin, Missouri, and Santa Fe in what was then Mexico, brought mules, jacks, and jennets of Spanish origin to Missouri while creating new markets for goods produced in Missouri. The Spanish jack stock, however, was small, producing mules good for pack animals but not large enough for heavy draft work.

The period from 1850 to 1900 saw a growing demand for mules and increasing numbers of them. It also saw the development of what came to be called the "Missouri mule." Because Missouri was on the edge of the frontier, it was in the

Mules have been harnessed for a variety of tasks. Hilda
and Louise (shown here) served as mascots for the University of Missouri–Columbia veterinary school. (State
Historical Society of Missouri, Columbia)

right place to supply large numbers of mules to freight
haulers, the military, and homesteaders heading west for
land. Many mules were also needed for Missouri's own agriculture and timber industries. Missouri bordered the cotton
belt, the largest market for Missouri's mules for many years.

Knowing they had to produce larger mules, Missouri breeders began scouring Kentucky and Tennessee for larger jacks,
particularly the American Mammoth variety, which had been
developed there. At the same time, large European-bred draft

1904 World's Fair Champion Mules. The press frequently referred to the "Missouri Mule" during the fair. (State Historical Society of Missouri, Columbia)

mares became more available. Breeders preferred the large, well-mannered French Percheron mares. By the end of the nineteenth century, the "real Missouri mule" could be defined: a black mule with white muzzle, well trained, and produced from a cross between a Mammoth jack and a Percheron mare. The term *Missouri mule* was used often by the press at the time of the 1904 St. Louis World's Fair.

Even though the highest prices were paid for larger mules, 1,200 to 1,400 pounds, Missouri continued to produce a number of smaller mules for specific markets. They produced many mules weighing between 900 and 1,150 pounds for the cotton industry. While the larger mules were ideal for heavy draft work such as dirt moving and logging, small mules were needed for some types of mining. Mule numbers increased dramatically between 1850 and 1900. Census figures show the United States mule population at 500,000 in 1850 and over 3 million in 1900. Mules have had a major economic impact on Missouri, having been sold to every other state and some foreign countries. During the time when mules were widely used, there were several large mule dealers in Missouri. Melvin Bradley tells of one such dealer, Guyton and Harrington, who sold $37,000,000 worth of mules to the British during World War I.

Mules have rendered tremendous service to mankind. They have performed all kinds of grueling work under harsh conditions. They have served in war, with many being killed during combat. Nearly every industry has employed mules in one way or another. Lead and coal have been extensively mined in Missouri, and mules have been used in Missouri's mining operations since the late 1700s. In open-pit coal mines, large, heavy mules were used, while smaller mules worked in underground mining. Small size was particularly important in coal seams, which are often little more than six feet high.

Mules have been widely used in agriculture, and Missouri has always been an agricultural state. Early farmers needed many large mules to plow, disc, plant, cultivate, and harvest crops on the deep prairie soils north of the Missouri River. In the Bootheel, the development of cotton farming meant that the planter needed a smaller mule, one able to cultivate cotton without stepping on too many plants.

Road and railroad building throughout the state and the construction of drainage ditches, particularly in southeast Missouri, required the use of large, powerful mules to haul dirt. The westward expansion of the nation also increased demand for Missouri mules. They carried freight and settlers headed west.

We think less often about the mule's military contributions than about its other uses. However, many mules, including large numbers from Missouri, have been used by the military. The proliferation of settlers and trading in the West increased the demand for large draft mules for military use. With the

This World War II B-26 bomber, named for the Missouri mule, was piloted by George Parker of Columbia (standing, left). (Collection of George Parker)

influx of settlers came the need to protect them and their property. This put new demands on the army, which began building forts in strategic locations throughout the West. The soldiers were totally dependent on military supply wagons for food, building material, weapons, and ammunition. Mules were the draft animals of choice to move these supplies. The military also employed large numbers of somewhat smaller mules as pack animals to transport supplies to troops in areas where roads were too poorly developed to use wagons.

Through World War II, mules served the military in every war in which our nation was engaged. They worked primarily as pack animals, carrying supplies and artillery. Although little attention has been given to military use of mules in World

War II, they were used in the Philippines, Burma, China, India, Italy, and other locations. In areas with either mountainous or wet, soggy terrain, roads could become impassable for mechanized units. Pack mules were the only means of getting supplies and artillery in to support infantry troops. The British and American military even experimented with airdrops of replacement pack mules into remote areas but stopped when many of the animals were injured. Animals in military service also suffered bullet and shrapnel wounds, starvation, dehydration, fatigue, parasites, and disease.

The advent of the internal combustion engine signaled the beginning of the end of the dominance of mules for hauling and draft work. By the 1920s, trucks had taken over much of the hauling. The '20s, '30s, and '40s saw tractors slowly begin to dominate farming operations. Many heated debates occurred over the relative merits of mules and tractors. For many farmers during the depression, economics made mule power the better choice. In the cash economy of the time, they did not have the money needed for changing to tractors and buying the gasoline necessary for their operation. But as tractors improved, it was inevitable that they would eventually replace mules as a primary power source on farms and in construction work. Tractors had taken over by the end of the 1940s.

Admirers of the mule remained, and mule breeding has continued. Although they are used less often than in the past, mules are by no means absent from the scene. Today they are used mainly for recreational purposes. Mule shows have become a popular attraction. There are several mule events at the Missouri State Fair each year, as well as at other events across Missouri and in other states. Field days feature demonstrations of working draft mules. The University of Missouri College of Veterinary Medicine has a mascot team of beautiful mules that has appeared all over the state. Mules frequently pull wagons in parades, and saddle mules are used in hunting and on trail rides.

Mule jumping is another popular event at shows. In this event, the mule must, from a standstill, jump over a barrier. The sport originated from the use of mules in raccoon hunting. Whenever the hunter encountered a fence, he would dismount, cover the fence with a blanket, and have the mule jump over the fence. The rider would then climb over the fence and remount. The practice of draping a blanket or tarp over the barrier to be jumped was developed to train the mule to jump only over a covered barrier. Otherwise, any mule taught to jump would be impossible to keep in its pasture at home. The current world champion jumping mule is from—where else?—Missouri.

Mules have survived many changes, including the shift in their duties. Even the preferred color of mules has changed. Although breeders have produced mules in many colors, for most of the mule's history in Missouri, black was the favored color. Now, however, sorrel mules are the most popular with mule fanciers.

Mules have contributed significantly to the settlement of the state and nation and have had a significant impact on the economy of Missouri. They served on the front line in times of war, and they continue to provide recreational enjoyment. They are strong and independent, yet dedicated, with a strong sense of self-preservation. All indications are that the Missouri mule will be around for us to enjoy for a long time. In 1995, it received the recognition it had long deserved when Representatives Jerry E. McBride and Mary C. Kasten introduced a bill, which was adopted by the state legislature and signed by Governor Mel Carnahan, naming the Missouri mule the state's official animal.

9

State Horse

Missouri Fox Trotting Horse

The Missouri fox trotting horse received official designation as the state horse June 4, 2002, when Governor Bob Holden signed legislation making it a new state symbol. Even before its official designation, the Missouri fox trotter was regarded as Missouri's horse, having been developed, early in the nineteenth century, in the Ozarks as a surefooted mount for working cattle in the rugged, rocky terrain. These horses, while used as all-around workhorses, were also attractive and showy when pulling the buggy or taking the owner to town.

Fossil records provide a relatively well documented history of the horse. The earliest ancestors developed in North America about fifty-five million years ago. The genus *Equus,* to which all modern horses and their relatives belong, was abundant in North and South America during the ice ages (two million to ten thousand years ago). Numerous fossilized remains have survived in glacial deposits in Missouri. During this time, horses migrated to Asia and from there spread over Europe and Africa. For reasons that are not understood, the horse became extinct in the Americas between eight and ten thousand years ago but flourished in Europe, Asia, and Africa.

Man's first contact with the horse was probably hunting it for food. Work by the Hartwick College Institute for Ancient Equestrian Studies (IAES) indicates that domestication began about 7,000 years ago when farmers kept horses for food. Nomadic groups next used horses as pack animals,

The Missouri fox trotting horse is both a surefooted worker and a graceful show horse. (Missouri State Archives)

making it much easier for them to move from place to place. Researchers at the IAES have also found evidence, through the study of bit wear on the teeth of ancient horses discovered in Russia, suggesting that horseback riding began 5,000 to 5,500 years ago in the steppes east of the Ural Mountains. From that time on, the use of the horse for transportation, warfare, and farming expanded.

From the end of the Ice Age until the 1500s, horses were absent from North America. During this time, Native Americans knew nothing about horses. The Spanish reintroduced the horse to America when explorers such as Coronado, Cortez, and DeSoto brought horses for their expeditions. DeSoto was perhaps the first to reach what is now Missouri. Horses that escaped from these and later explorers formed the first of the wild herds that still roam parts of the western United States.

The 1600s ushered in the breeding of horses for specific purposes both in Europe and America. Large horses with a soft, easy gait that made riding more comfortable were the norm in most of Europe. The Moors from North Africa introduced the lighter, faster Arabian and other similar types to Spain. These various bloodlines provided the genetics for developing diverse breeds.

Rhode Island was the major horse-breeding region in America from the mid-1600s to the mid-1700s. Virginia then became a horse-breeding center, followed by Kentucky and Tennessee. The combined efforts in these areas gave rise to several distinctive American horse breeds, including Narragansett pacers (now extinct), Thoroughbreds, Morgans, American saddlebreds, standardbreds, and Tennessee walking horses. Bloodlines from these breeds contributed to the development of today's Missouri fox trotting horse.

As settlers moved westward from Virginia, Kentucky, Tennessee, and Illinois into the Ozarks of Missouri and Arkansas, they brought with them excellent horses. However, the rocky, forested hills presented special challenges for settlers using horses to herd cattle. Most horses are lateral gaited, that is, they move the feet on one side at the same time (left front and left rear–right front and right rear). The settlers discovered that horses that were diagonal gaited (left front and right rear–right front and left rear) provided a much smoother ride and were more surefooted in the difficult, rugged terrain. This diagonal gait is the movement referred to as the fox trot, which these horses can maintain over long distances. The appearance of this gait is described by the Missouri Fox Trotting Horse Breed Association as walking with the front feet and trotting with the rear. The back feet are moved in a sliding manner, which accounts for the minimal jarring experienced by the rider.

As the fox trotter's popularity grew, selective breeding increased their numbers. Ozark settlers utilized fox trotters not only for working cattle, but also for pulling plows and buggies. The U.S. Forest Service has also frequently chosen to use them. While the surefooted fox trotters give a smooth ride, they also display a gentle disposition and intelligence, making them easy to train and to handle. Today, these traits are once more increasing the breed's popularity. The Missouri fox trotting horse is now a favorite for trail rides as well as a dependable worker for cattlemen and a star of the showring, where it performs its three gaits: flat-foot walk, fox trot, and canter.

The Missouri Fox Trotting Horse Breed Association, headquartered in Ava, maintains the registry for the breed. They hold an annual six-day fox trotting horse show and celebration along with other events during the year on the association grounds. Registration began in 1948, when a group of interested breeders formed an organization. The group reorganized in 1973, becoming a membership corporation. Registration books were kept open until January 1982, after which at least one parent had to be already registered. Starting in January 1983, to be registered as a Missouri fox trotter, both parents of the candidate had to be registered. The association now has over 8,000 members and more than 60,300 horses registered.

Upon urging from the Missouri Fox Trotting Horse Breed Association, Representative Van Kelly of Norwood sponsored a bill in the 2002 legislative session to name this outstanding breed Missouri's state horse. With its ever increasing popularity as a pleasure and cross-country trail-riding horse, in addition to its able performance as a show horse and continued service to cattlemen, the Missouri fox trotter has secured its place of prominence in the world of horses.

10

State Fish

Channel Catfish

The idea for a state fish came from the Mid-America 4-H Wildlife Club of Elkland in Webster County. First, the club put together a survey to see what other Missourians thought. Members of the club placed survey forms in sporting goods stores and the *Missouri Conservationist* among other places. Missourians apparently had quite a few thoughts about fish, and because of survey results, the state of Missouri actually acquired two new symbols. The group asked Representative Kenneth Legan of Halfway in Polk County to sponsor legislation designating the channel catfish (*Ictalurus punctatus*) the state fish and the paddlefish (*Polydon spathula*) the state aquatic animal. Representative Marilyn A. Williams cosponsored the bill, which was signed by Governor Mel Carnahan May 23, 1997.

Channel catfish have a streamlined, sleek appearance, and they, along with one other type of catfish in Missouri, have deeply forked tails. Their smooth, scaleless skin is bluish gray on the sides, sometimes with greenish yellow shading, while their undersides are creamy white. Catfish have some good defenses. Both their dorsal and pectoral fins, located just behind the gills, have a very sharp spine that can inflict a painful wound. They also have distinctive barbels around the mouth, which are suggestive of a cat's whiskers, thus their name. Channel catfish have eight of these sensory organs, which help the fish locate food. They contain taste

The channel catfish is a favorite of both anglers and fish farmers. (Missouri Department of Conservation, photo by Jim Rathert)

buds, enabling the catfish to "taste" their food before they eat it and also aiding them in finding food in turbid water where sight is restricted.

Channel catfish tend to stay in cover and deep water during the day. At night, they venture into shallow areas to feed. Their diet includes other fish, insects, crayfish, mollusks, and some plant material. These fish are called "channel" catfish because they more often inhabit swifter water in rivers and streams than do other catfish. They also flourish in backwater areas along rivers as well as in lakes and ponds. Spawning occurs between the last week of May and the third week of July. The male selects a nesting site around hollow logs, undercut banks, or other natural cavities. After the female deposits the eggs, the male stands guard until the young fish leave the nest. Channel catfish typically mature in about four or five years at twelve to fifteen inches long. They commonly weigh one to five pounds, although they can grow much larger; the Missouri state record fish, weighing thirty-four pounds, ten ounces, was caught in Lake Jacomo by Gerald Siebenmorgen. The national record channel catfish weighed fifty-eight pounds and was caught in South Carolina.

The channel catfish, one of the state's top sport fish, is abundant throughout the state. It is particularly common in the Missouri and Mississippi Rivers as well as streams in north and west Missouri and the lowland waters in the southeastern part of the state. The channel catfish is both a strong fighting fish to catch and an excellent tasting fish to eat. Because of their natural tendency to eat just about anything, they can be caught with a wide variety of bait, including artificial lures. They are caught with line- and pole-fishing methods and also with set lines. The latter method consists of lines that are attached between stakes set in the water or tied to the bank, an overhanging limb, or a jug floating in the water. Every catfisherman has his own favorite bait. Since catfish feed by smell as much as by sight, some of these baits consist of some rather foul-smelling concoctions, such as strong cheese and chicken liver. This type of bait is available commercially. Other popular baits are worms and minnows.

The channel catfish is a major commercial fish as well as a top sport fish in Missouri. It makes up a large portion of the fish harvested for sale from Missouri's waterways. The production of channel catfish in ponds for the restaurant and grocery store market has become a large industry. Channel catfish are well suited to fish farming. They can tolerate wide variations in water temperature and high populations; they grow rapidly, and they use food efficiently. Aquaculture is the fastest growing area of agriculture. Catfish farming is a specialized industry in which the fish are raised in ponds where the water quality and feed rations are closely monitored. In 1998, sales by catfish farms totaled $469 million nationwide. Missouri farm-raised catfish had a value of $2,130,000 in 1999, making Missouri fifth in the nation in aquaculture.

While not everyone who took part in the original survey agreed that the channel catfish should be the state fish (many liked the large-mouth bass), the channel catfish excels in every aspect in representing Missouri. It is abundant in most of the state's waterways and is the fish of choice for Missouri's growing aquaculture industry.

11

State Aquatic Animal
Paddlefish

House Bill 700, naming the channel catfish as Missouri's state fish, also recognized a second fish as a state symbol. The bill designated the paddlefish (*Polydon spathula*) the state aquatic animal on May 23, 1997. Whether it is called a fish or an aquatic animal, the paddlefish is certainly unique enough to have official recognition.

The paddlefish is commonly known by several other names, including spoonbill, spoonbill cat, and shovelnose cat, because it has been mistakenly thought by some to be a member of the catfish family. Its most distinctive feature is its long, flat, paddlelike snout. The paddlefish, which does not have scales, is bluish gray on its upper part and nearly white on its belly. It is a large fish that grows rapidly. One may reach 10 to 14 inches in its first year and 21 inches by its second year, and some may grow to 160 pounds. The Missouri state record weight is 134 pounds, 12 ounces, for a paddlefish caught in Lake of the Ozarks in March 1998. Paddlefish exceeding 60 pounds are frequently caught. They are also long-lived fish, with some living as long as 30 years.

Besides appearance and size, the paddlefish is unique in other ways. Its skeleton is made not of bone, but of cartilage, like the skeletons of sharks and sturgeon. Paddlefish also feed in an unusual manner. Lacking teeth, they feed on plankton, which are microscopic organisms in the water, by swimming around with their mouths wide open. They filter

The paddlefish is easily recognized by its bill. (Missouri Department of Conservation, photo by Jim Rathert)

water through gill rakers to remove the food organisms, then expel the water. Missouri's paddlefish are members of an ancient and rare order of fishes; there is only one other member, another type of paddlefish that lives in China. Fossils indicate that the paddlefish was present three hundred million years ago, before the dinosaurs.

Paddlefish normally live in the open waters of large lakes and rivers, but they change locations for spawning. They do not appear to have a definite home territory and travel great distances when feeding. Spawning occurs when the water temperature has reached fifty degrees Farenheit in the spring. The adults migrate upstream to gravel and sandbars covered by very shallow water, where eggs are deposited and fertilized. Newly hatched paddlefish require rising water from floods to carry them off the bars and into deeper water. This spawning process was not well understood until it was observed by biologists on the Osage River, upstream from Lake of the Ozarks, in 1960.

Before 1900, large populations of paddlefish existed throughout the Mississippi and Missouri River valleys. Construction of dams, stream channelization, and drainage of bottomland lakes have contributed to the loss of suitable habitat for paddlefish feeding and reproduction. Historically, the greatest populations in Missouri have been in the Mississippi, Missouri, and Osage Rivers. One of the largest paddlefish populations in the United States has been in Lake of the Ozarks and the upper Osage River. Ideal habitat existed there until 1977, when construction of the Truman Dam flooded most of the paddlefish spawning areas on the Osage. Populations are now maintained there and in other areas through stocking programs.

The function of the paddlefish's bill has been the subject of considerable speculation. Some have suggested that it is used to stir up sediment along the bottom to search for food. However, no one has observed this, and it is inconsistent with the way paddlefish feed. Studies by Lon Wilkens of the University of Missouri–St. Louis have shown that paddlefish use electroreceptors on their paddles, gill covers, and the tops of their heads to detect weak electrical fields that are produced by plankton. These receptors aid paddlefish in finding food.

In *Fishes of Missouri,* William L. Pflieger states that at the end of the nineteenth century the paddlefish was the most important commercial fish in the Mississippi Valley, not only for its flesh, but also for its eggs, which were sold as caviar. The commercial harvest of paddlefish in Missouri is now small, with most caught in trammel nets. The paddlefish continues to be a sport fish, although fishing for paddlefish requires a different method than fishing for other species. Paddlefish will not bite bait. Consequently, they are caught by snagging during the spring spawning season in areas where their numbers are concentrated. Snagging is accomplished

by attaching one or two large treble hooks to a strong mono-
filament line. The line is then either cast or trolled behind a
boat, and the fish are snagged by one of the hooks.

Hatcheries have successfully reared paddlefish for stocking, thus helping to reduce some of the devastating effects of
habitat loss on the paddlefish population. This ancient and
unique fish, which once filled Missouri's waterways, is a fitting
symbol of the state's aquatic wildlife.

12

State Insect

Honeybee

The dog has often been called man's best friend. However, when the value of its contribution to the world's food supply through pollination is considered, the honeybee (*Apis mellifera*) has to rank close to the top of a list of creatures beneficial to man. In recognition of its importance, the honeybee was named the state insect on July 3, 1985. The Missouri State Beekeepers Association, under the leadership of Flernoy Jones, state apiculture specialist at that time, made the proposal to the state legislature. Missouri has not been the only state to recognize the value of this insect. The honeybee could be considered the king of state insects. Sixteen states have honored this flying marvel by naming it either state insect or state agricultural insect.

Despite the high esteem in which it is held in this country, the honeybee is not native to the Americas. It arrived here via settlers from Europe. The American Indians referred to honeybees as "white man's flies." Honeybees were one of the first items England shipped to its New World colonies. As early as the 1620s, bees had arrived in Virginia. Within a few years, they were present in all settled areas. They probably originated in Africa and spread from there to Europe, India, and China. They have not changed much. Fossilized bees that lived thirty million years ago appear nearly identical to modern bees.

The products that honeybees provide, honey and beeswax,

Honeybees are excellent pollinators. (Missouri Department of Conservation, photo by Jim Rathert)

have been staples for centuries. The Bible makes fifty-six references to honey, which has been used not only as a sweetener, but also as an antiseptic. In ancient times, it was sometimes applied to a wound to aid in healing. The antiseptic benefits result from honey's acidity, the concentrated sugars (which cause water to be drawn out of bacteria cells), and the small amount of hydrogen peroxide, a widely used antiseptic, present. Fermented honey was used to make a beverage in several ancient cultures. Beeswax has many uses: It has been used as a sealing wax; as an ingredient in lubricants, furniture polishes, and cosmetics bases; to make candles and a painting medium; and in the casting of statues. Candle making has created the largest demand for beeswax. Even today, the finest candles are made from beeswax.

Today, most honey is sold in liquid form, packaged in a variety of containers for home use or shipped in bulk containers for commercial use in baking, candy making, and producing honey butter. According to the Missouri Agricultural Statistics Service, the state produces about 1.5 million pounds of honey each year. Honey sells for seventy to eighty cents per pound, amounting to over one million dollars annually for honey sold.

Honeybees have a complex social structure. A typical hive will contain between thirty thousand and sixty thousand bees in the summer. Honeybees are divided into three classes: queens, drones, and workers. Each hive usually contains only one queen. The first new queen to hatch kills all unhatched queens and often kills the old queen. She then leaves the hive and is pursued by many drones, both from her hive and other hives. She will mate with several drones over two or three days. After mating, the drones die. The queen may return to her original hive to replace the old queen or be followed by some of the workers from that hive to start a new one. The drone's sperm are stored by the queen and are used over a lifespan of three or four years to fertilize eggs as they are laid. An egg that is not fertilized will develop into a drone or male. The queen spends her entire life laying eggs and producing chemicals called pheromones. These chemical scents basically control the behavior of workers. New queens are produced when fertilized eggs are placed by workers in a larger comb cell. This larger cell provides room needed for the queen larva. This larva is fed special food called royal jelly produced by the special glands on worker bees.

Workers, which develop from fertilized eggs, are females that have diminished ovaries but develop stingers and venom pouches. The workers are the only bees that can sting. Ironically, after the stinger penetrates its victim, the bee cannot pull it back. The stinger pulls out of the bee's abdomen, and the bee dies.

Worker bees have a host of duties. They feed the larvae and the queen, clean and defend the hive, build comb, and gather nectar, pollen, and plant resins. Workers even have a complex communication system, which consists of dances performed by foraging workers upon returning to the hive. These dances communicate to other workers both the distance and direction to a food source. Bees collect nectar from flowers to make honey. The nectar, which is mostly water and sucrose, is stored in each bee's crop, an organ located in its abdomen. There, special chemicals called enzymes convert it to glucose and fructose. This modified nectar is then carried to the hive and stored in a cell in the comb. In the hive, other workers fan their wings to evaporate some of the water until the moisture content of the honey is about 18 percent. Bees in a hive will travel over fifty-five thousand miles to collect enough nectar for one pound of honey. A worker will collect about one-twelfth of a teaspoon of honey during its adult life, which is about six weeks.

Bees also collect pollen and propolis from plants. Pollen collection benefits both bees and plants because as the bees gather they pollinate the plants. Pollen, which is mixed with honey in the hive and stored in cells, is a source of protein for the bees. Propolis is composed of gums and resins collected from tree buds and stored in a special area on the workers' third pair of legs. It is used like varnish to coat the inside of the hive and seal cracks. Beeswax, made from wax scales produced by the bees' wax glands, is used to build the comb.

Beekeepers have steadily improved their equipment and techniques. Apiculturists must use good management practices to keep their hives producing. This includes control of pests, moving hives to better areas for bees to forage for nectar and pollen, and supplemental feeding during the winter. Until the movable frame was developed in 1852, bees were kept in a variety of hives made of wood, straw, or pottery. Such hives made bees difficult to manage. Often it was necessary to kill the bees in the fall to remove the honey and beeswax. The movable frames made it possible to harvest honey or wax without destroying the hive. Other innovations, such as the smoker and centrifugal honey extractor, soon

Beehive harvesting.
(State Historical
Society of Missouri,
Columbia)

followed. Another beekeeping improvement was the intro-
duction of an Italian strain of bees. These bees tended to be
less excitable and more resistant to disease.

One particularly difficult problem beekeepers have faced
since the 1980s is tracheal mites. These parasites live in
the breathing tubes of bees and can kill entire bee colonies.
Another problem mite is the varroa. These mites suck blood
from both adult and developing bees. Untreated, they can
also destroy entire colonies. Both pests have caused significant financial losses for the bee industry in recent years. A
number of bacterial and viral diseases can also cause diffi-
culties for beekeepers.

Perhaps the most valuable service honeybees provide is pollination, which is secondary to their primary activities of gathering nectar and pollen. Good pollination of flowers contributes enormously to the production of both wild and cultivated plants. A wide variety of crops are partially or totally dependent on bee pollination for production of abundant, high-quality crops. Pollination is the transfer of pollen from the anthers of a flower to the stigma. After a pollen grain is placed on the stigma, it germinates, forming a tube that grows into the ovary where a sperm cell is then released for fertilization.

Some flowers contain both the male (anther) and female (ovary) parts. In others, male and female parts are on different flowers on the same plant, and in some they occur on different plants. Unless pollen is transferred so that fertilization can occur, the plants will not bear fruit. Wind and insects are the primary means of distributing pollen. Honeybees are particularly suited to this task because they forage for pollen to feed the large number of bees in a colony. In addition, honeybees will go from one flower to another of the same kind as long as it is available.

In an article in *Bee Culture* magazine, Roger A. Morse and Nicholas W. Calderone, both of Cornell University, estimate that $14.6 billion in increased yield and quality of crops in the United States can be attributed to pollination by honeybees. Recognizing the value of pollination, growers often pay beekeepers to place hives near their crops during peak bloom periods. Neal Bergman, owner of Delta Bee Company, in Kennett, one of the largest beekeeping businesses in Missouri, has even transported hives as far away as California to pollinate almond trees. Renting out hives in this manner produces additional income for the beekeeper.

Considering its contributions of honey, beeswax, and beneficial pollination, the honeybee seems to live up to the adage "busy as a bee." This amazing creature is well deserving of its title: Missouri state insect.

13

State Song

"Missouri Waltz"

Hush-a-bye, ma baby, slumbertime is comin' soon;
Rest yo' head upon my breast while Mommy hums
    a tune;
The Sandman is callin' where shadows are fallin',
While the soft breezes sigh as in days long gone by.

So begin the lyrics of Missouri's nostalgic state song, but for all its surface charm, the song has a murky history and is an unusual choice for a state song. There were numerous attempts to find a suitable state song prior to 1949, when the present song was adopted, but Missourians seem to have had a difficult time reaching a decision on this matter. A Missourian in the presidency aroused interest again in finding a state song, and the "Missouri Waltz," which many thought was President Harry Truman's favorite, was chosen.

Many songs and poems have been written through the years extolling various virtues of Missouri and Missourians. In 1900, an article in the *Jefferson City Missouri State Tribune* generated some interest in the selection of a state song. The paper printed a song called "Missouri" with words by D. E. Grayson and music by B. J. Writsman. But after this initial show of interest, the *Tribune* did nothing else to promote this song.

The first concerted effort in this direction came in the fall of 1908, when the Daughters of the American Revolution announced a contest to find a Missouri state song. In Nov-

65

In 1995 residents of Howard County dedicated a grave marker for Lee Edgar Settle, "composer of the 'Missouri Waltz,'" in Mt. Pleasant Cemetery near New Franklin. Ragtime musicians had performed at a benefit concert to raise funds for the marker two years earlier. (Missouri State Archives)

ember of 1909, they selected three songs from twenty-six submitted. The three were to be sung at their next state meeting. For some unknown reason, the judges, selected by the song committee, took no action. In the fall of 1909, Governor Herbert S. Hadley initiated a contest to find a state song, securing prize money of five hundred dollars each for lyrics and music. He named a committee to organize the contest and select a panel of judges. Under chairman W. H. Pommer of the University of Missouri, the panel announced official rules, which required that all rights be transferred to the state. The closing date for the contest was October 31, 1910. The contest drew entries from every state as well as Canada and Australia.

Pommer sorted through the 1,013 submissions and presented 73 to the judges. The decision was announced by Governor Hadley on May 15, 1911. Lizzie Chambers Hull of St. Louis had won the five hundred dollar lyrics prize for her poem, "Missouri." None of the music submitted, however, was judged suitable. The contest for music was opened September 30 and closed November 30, 1911.

Pommer had selected one hundred songs from those submitted for the judges to consider. Meeting on February 28, 1912, the judges reduced the number of contenders to four. After several hours of consideration, they could not reach a consensus about the four so they called the governor in what may have been one of the first teleconferences in the state. The judges played and sang the four compositions into the telephone so the governor could hear them. Governor Hadley could not decide either. He had the four songs circulated among glee clubs around the state and suggested that the most popular win the five hundred dollars. This plan also failed to produce a definite favorite, so no final decision was ever made.

The Missouri Daughters of the American Revolution held a contest in 1913 to find music to go with the words of Lizzie Hull's poem. They selected music composed by Julie Stevens Bacon and adopted this as their official state song. In 1913, the legislature considered a song entitled "Missouri" by Anna Brosius Korn, but it took no formal action. Between 1927 and 1931 the legislature looked at seven possibilities for a state song but accepted none. The house gave approval to "Missouri" by Lizzie Hull and Noel Poepping in 1933, but the senate failed to vote on it. The house again considered this song in 1935 but did not vote. "Missouri" by Gertie Colvin and "Missouri" by Lizzie Hull, both without music, appeared on the senate calendar in 1937, but neither bill got further than a first reading.

Harry Truman's becoming president in 1945 renewed interest in a state song. The "Missouri Waltz" was played at the

Potsdam Conference, which Truman attended. Thus, the song became associated with him and perhaps stirred interest in it as the state song. Floyd Snyder of Independence sponsored a bill in 1949 to name "Missouri Waltz" the state song. During the discussion, Snyder stated that it was Truman's favorite song. The original lyrics contained some objectionable words. Representative James Neal from Kansas City, one of four African American members of the general assembly, proposed an amendment calling for the replacement of the words "pickaninny," "Mammy," and "darkies," which appeared in the original version, with "little child," "Mommy," and "old folks," respectively. Both the house and the senate accepted the amended version. Finally, on June 30, 1949, Missouri had an official state song.

While the origins and composer of the "Missouri Waltz" are uncertain, it was first published in 1912 by Frederick Knight Logan of Oskaloosa, Iowa. He published one thousand copies in Chicago and circulated them among bandleaders and music dealers. The lyrics did not appear with this first publication. A couple of years later, Logan sold rights to the piece to F. J. A. Forster for one hundred dollars. Forster published it again, this time with lyrics supposedly written by James Shannon, who was paid one hundred dollars. When first published, the title was "Hush-a-Bye Ma Baby" with "Missouri Waltz" appearing in parentheses. The song was slow to sell at first, but by 1939 it had sold nearly six million copies. For a number of years it was the second largest selling sheet music in the nation.

There are numerous versions of the origins of the "Missouri Waltz." Frederick Logan, the first publisher of the song, apparently obtained it from John Eppel, a bandleader from Fort Dodge, Iowa. From there the story becomes cloudy. Relatives of Lee Edgar Settle, a talented piano player from New Franklin, claimed that he was the composer. He called the song "Graveyard Waltz" and never put the music on paper. The story goes that he was playing it in Moberly and was overheard by John Eppel, who wrote the music as Settle played. Another version of this story is that Settle obtained the melody from the DiArmo sisters, a musical group he toured with, who, in turn, got it from an old African American man in the South. Yet another version of the story says that Eppel got the song from an African American woman he met while touring the South, and another, that an Eppel heard it from an African American violin player in Sedalia. In the Moberly area, some say that that Dab Hannah, an African American piano player, was the composer. Whatever its origin, the "Missouri Waltz" became a popular song and is well accepted as the official state song even though Missouri is only mentioned twice in the composition.

Was the "Missouri Waltz" really a favorite song of Harry Truman's? Apparently not. Although he even played it at the White House, a few quotes from Missouri's president seem to indicate that he was not fond of the song. While the song was being considered in the Missouri General Assembly, a White House representative was asked whether or not the song was really the president's favorite. The response from the White House: "President's attitude towards the song? He can take it or leave it. Is it really his favorite? No. Does he play it often? No. Is Margaret ever heard singing it? No. What is the President's reaction to the song's adoption by Missouri as state song? See answer to first question."

In a television interview President Truman said: "If you let me say what I think, I don't give a ———— about it, but I can't say it out loud because it's the song of Missouri. It's as bad as the 'The Star Spangled Banner' as far as music is concerned." The famous bandleader Guy Lombardo responded by saying that the "Missouri Waltz" was "one of the finest melodies ever written." Years after leaving office, Truman was asked again if the "Missouri Waltz" was his favorite song. He responded, "You ought to read the words and then you'd see why it's kind of obnoxious as a state song."

14

State Musical Instrument

Fiddle

When the first French fur traders plied the waters of the Mississippi and Missouri Rivers and the first settlers from Virginia, the Carolinas, Tennessee, and other southeastern states crossed the Mississippi River looking for new land, they brought their cultures with them. Music was a part of those cultures, and the fiddle provided much of that music. Centuries later, from the rolling prairie land of northern Missouri across the Ozarks to the hills around Branson, the sound of the fiddle can still be heard in many settings. The instrument has filled a major role in the state's musical heritage, and it became our official musical instrument on July 17, 1987.

The fiddle has long been part of many cultures. The earliest records of instruments played with a bow came from Persia in the ninth century. These early instruments took many shapes and sizes. Fiddles seem to have shown up in Europe in the tenth century. The classical violin began to develop in Italy during the sixteenth century, but fiddles became a part of the folk culture in much of Europe and were very popular in Scotland and Ireland. This heritage, which emigrants from these areas brought with them to America, has strongly influenced American folk music.

The question is often raised as to the difference between a fiddle and a violin. From a historical perspective, we might say that violins are fiddles, but not all fiddles are violins. Studying word origins helps resolve this dilemma. The word

The fiddle was brought to Missouri by the early French fur traders, and French tunes are still played in Ste. Genevieve and the old mining areas. Today Missouri is known around the world for its distinctive fiddling styles, according to old-time fiddling expert Howard Marshall. (Photo by Don Lance)

fiddle was derived from the Middle English word *fidele,* itself derived from the medieval Latin word *vitula. Violin* is a diminutive form of the Italian word *viola,* derived from the same medieval Latin term as fiddle, *vitula.* Traditionally, the fiddle has been associated with folk music while the violin has been associated with classical music. Today, they are the same instrument played in different ways. Fiddle players often use different tuning techniques than those used in standard violin tuning. Different techniques produce distinctly different sounds. Variations in the techniques used to draw the bow across the strings also produce unique sounds.

As immigrants came to America from many parts of the world, bringing with them their music, the fiddle became a

Devin Quick of Fulton enjoys fiddling sessions with some of Missouri's traditional fiddlers at the Boone County Historical Museum in Columbia. (Photo by Don Lance)

popular instrument from New England to Georgia. Thomas Jefferson was reportedly an accomplished fiddler. Local craftsman began making fiddles, experimenting with various woods and finishes as they designed and constructed the instrument. As the westward migration began, traders, explorers, and settlers took their music, which was becoming a blend of many traditions, with them. The fiddle, being lightweight and small, was easily transported on the journey westward. Thus, the fiddle was one of the first instruments to cross the Appalachian Mountains and the Mississippi River into the western frontier. A letter written by Francis O'Neill in November 1906 and published in the *Journal of the Irish Folk Song* illustrates how numerous and popular fiddlers were in nineteenth-century Missouri: "As many as nine attended one dance, I remember. Fiddlers in Missouri and other middle and western states were as numerous as harpers in eighteenth century Ireland."

The fiddle has always been associated with dance, whether Irish jigs, waltzes, polkas, clogging, or square dancing. However, in some areas of Missouri, religious fervor in the late nineteenth and early twentieth centuries caused people to refer to the fiddle as "the devil's box," presumably because of its association with dancing, good times, and, in some settings, strong drink. The fiddle was frequently a part of social events such as informal Sunday afternoon gatherings or Saturday night town dances, creating a steady demand for the services of a good fiddler. These musical gatherings also helped relieve some of the stress in early settlers' lives. R. P. Christeson, writing in *The Old Time Fiddlers Repertory,* published by the University of Missouri Press, recalls: "This is how people would lay aside their troubles and rekindle their energies. In addition to dances, there were musical gatherings where the hearing and playing of these old tunes would help dissolve fatigue. Fiddle music made a definite contribution toward the amelioration of a harsh and difficult existence and fostered neighborliness among many people."

Styles of fiddle playing and the songs performed varied from one region of the country to another and even from one part of a state to another, depending largely on the ethnic heritage of early settlers in that region. For example, around Ste. Genevieve and into the old lead belt to the west, the old-time fiddlers played songs of French origin that weren't generally known elsewhere. In the central part of the state, along the Missouri River, there was significant German settlement in the 1800s, and, as expected, fiddling there showed a strong German influence. The Ozarks, the area of the state known as "Little Dixie" (which includes Boone, Callaway, Clay, Cooper, Howard, Lafayette, and Saline Counties), and the Missouri Valley in the northwestern part of the state all have distinctive fiddling styles. The Scotch-Irish style, as well as others, have influenced fiddling in these areas. Three Missouri fiddlers from different cultural groups have received National Heritage Fellows awards from the National Endowment for the Arts: Lyman Enloe, "Old-Time" fiddler of Lee's Summit; Claude Williams, African American jazz/swing fiddler of Kansas City; and Bob Holt, Ozark fiddler from Ava.

Fiddling contests are a main venue for the performance of old-time fiddle music today, and there are over eighty fiddle contests held each year in Missouri. The contests focus on older, traditional types of music. Rules require contestants to play specific types of songs, and judges score on a point system. Fiddling contests gained momentum in the mid-1920s when Henry Ford, of automobile fame, became interested in preserving traditional fiddle music. He sponsored numerous contests, which greatly increased the fiddle's popularity. The Missouri State Fiddle Championship is conducted by the Missouri State Old Time Fiddlers Association at the Missouri State Fair each year.

The fiddle represents the traditional music of Missouri. Its varied sounds can still be heard at jam sessions, contests, dances, and other programs throughout the state. Brought to the state by the first traders and settlers three centuries ago, the fiddle remains an important part of the state's cultural heritage.

15

State American Folk Dance

Square Dance

"Allemande left, circle to the right, promenade home." These are a few of the many calls that keep square dancers on the move. Modern square dances are lively affairs with flashy dress, fun, and friendship. They continue centuries-old traditions. What we recognize as square dance today does not have a single origin but rather is a blend of influences spanning time and geography. The square dance became the official state American folk dance in Missouri on May 31, 1995. It had actually been adopted as the official national folk dance much earlier. In 1982, President Reagan signed a bill making that designation.

The lines of origin of the square dance are not clear and direct. Rather, this folk art was shaped by a wide array of influences. Dance itself is one of mankind's oldest art forms, originating perhaps in man's attempts to imitate the movement and action of animals. The dominant influences on folk dance in the United States were English and French. However, Scottish, Irish, and Spanish dances also contributed to the evolution of square dance.

One of the oldest dances influencing square dance was the morris dance of fifteenth-century England. It was a "long ways" dance, that is, two lines of male dancers (six in all) faced each other. Each dancer had a leather pad of bells tied around the calf of each leg. It was a vigorous, athletic dance. Later, English country dances developed that were danced

Square dances are lively affairs. (Missouri State Archives)

by couples on lawns and began with the dancers arranged in either lines or circles. These dances became very popular both in England and France.

In the 1600s, two French dances became popular. The first was a round dance called a branle. This was a ballroom dance of the aristocracy. The minuet, an aristocratic court dance, first appeared about this time as well and remained popular for centuries. Near the close of the seventeenth century, the English country dances made their way across the English Channel to France and became very popular there. In 1650, John Playford published a book of country dances, enhancing their popularity in both France and England. The French modified these English country dances into what became "contra-dance," meaning that the dancers were in lines opposite one another. By the eighteenth century, the French had further adapted the country dances into sets that consisted of four couples forming a square. These were the quadrilles and cotillion dances. By this point, a true square dance had evolved. The quadrille even featured a "promoter" to announce the next dance. This was the forerunner of the caller, which is a purely American development in square dance history.

At the same time the French were developing the quadrille, the country dances in England were evolving into squares for eight as well. As America was now being settled, all of these blended forms were ready for transport across the Atlantic. Because of the Puritans' influence, dancing was slow to catch on in New England. Early in the 1700s, however, a New England dance developed that was a combination of English country and French court dances. It was danced in the form of a square, a style developed in Virginia and the Carolinas that was much like an English country dance. However, it had very fast, active movements suggestive of morris dancing. This style came to be called the Appalachian Mountain dance. The merging of these two styles of folk dances is the foundation of modern square dancing.

From the Revolutionary War until the late 1800s, America was a nation of dancers. Just about any occasion could be reason for a dance. Husking bees, barn raisings, sheepshearings, and other events that brought a community together might be celebrated with a dance when the work was finished. The services of a caller and good fiddler were always in demand. Dances were held in many locations, including taverns, town meeting halls, barns, or private homes. At times, dances could become rowdy affairs. The combination of strong drink and competition for the attention of an attractive young woman sometimes led to fights and even knifings. This is an image of square dances that modern square dance clubs have worked hard to change.

Particularly in the Midwest during the late 1800s and early 1900s, there was much religious opposition to dances. Instead of dances, "play parties" were held. At these parties, the same movements and same songs would be used as in dances, but

Square dancing at the capitol. (Missouri State Archives)

no fiddle music was allowed. Only singing and clapping accompanied the games. It was during this period that the fiddle came to be called the "devil's instrument" or the "devil's music box" in some areas. There were strict standards of conduct at play parties. A young man was not allowed to put his arms around a girl's waist, and no alcoholic drinks were permitted.

By the mid-1920s, American folk dances were nearly lost. Henry Ford became interested in preserving some of this heritage. He employed a dance master, Benjamin Lovett, and began programs for teaching folk dances. He also built a dance hall and published a book of dances with Lovett. Lloyd Shaw, a school superintendent in Colorado, also became interested in researching American folk dances and published a book, *Cowboy Dances,* in 1939. Shaw trained teams of dancers to do exhibitions around the country. This revived an interest in square dance and other folk dances.

Square dancing began to change in the 1950s. New calls were developed, and recorded, rather than live, music began being used for dances. A wider variety of music began to be included. Microphones allowed one caller to call for large groups rather than one caller for each square as had sometimes been necessary at large dances in the past.

A major development for square dance was the establishment in 1974 of an organization known as CALLERLAB, the International Association of Square Dance Callers. One of its goals has been to standardize square dance terminology and calls. This would make it possible for members from one club to understand the calls and dance with members of any other club in the world.

With roots in England and France, square dancing in one form or another has been around many centuries. It has always been a popular pastime in Missouri and represents an important part of the state's folk history. Today, with over 180 square and round dance clubs in the state holding regular dances, square dancing appears to have a bright future.

16

State Mineral

Galena

The subject of mining often conjures up images of the mountainous regions of the western United States. While there has been and continues to be much mining activity there, Missouri can also be called a mining state. It hosts one of a relatively few mining schools in the nation, the University of Missouri–Rolla, formerly known as the Missouri School of Mines and Metallurgy. A number of materials are mined in Missouri, but the product that has become almost synonymous with the state is lead. Actually, lead is not mined. Rather, an ore mineral, galena, containing lead is mined and then refined to produce pure lead. The southeast Missouri mining district contains the largest known concentration of galena in the world. This abundance of galena has historically made Missouri a leading national and international lead producer.

Galena is an attractive metallic gray mineral that easily breaks into small cubes when struck. It frequently forms as crystals that are also usually cubic. The chemical formula for galena is PbS, lead sulfide. Copper, zinc, and silver sometimes occur as impurities in galena in amounts large enough to be recovered during the refining process. Currently, these metals are obtained when galena from Missouri mines is processed.

Lead mining has a long history in Missouri. The first to exploit this resource were the early French explorers in southeast Missouri. Around 1721, Philippe Francois Renault

Galena is mined to produce lead. (Geological Sciences, University of Missouri–Columbia, photo by Claudia Powell.)

began using slave labor to mine surface and near-surface deposits north of what is now Potosi. Mining also began about this same time at Mine La Motte near Fredericktown. During the early 1800s, Moses Austin began deeper mining near Potosi. Lead mining spread into the present counties of Washington, Jefferson, Madison, and St. Francois. In 1864, St. Joseph Lead Company was incorporated and began operations near Bonne Terre. Several other companies moved into this area, primarily St. Francois, Washington, and Madison Counties. Mining operations resulted in the founding of Flat River, Elvins, Rivermines, Leadwood, Desloge, Esther, Leadington, Doe Run, and Bonne Terre. This region of Missouri has become known as the Old Lead Belt. St. Joe became the largest operator in the Old Lead Belt and developed a series of mines that were connected by 250 miles of underground railroads.

As ore reserves began to decline in the Old Lead Belt, a discovery near Viburnum in Iron County opened a new area of mining. This area, known as the Viburnum Trend, is located south and west of the Old Lead Belt. The first ore production from this deposit was at St. Joseph's No. 27 mine in Crawford County in mid-1960s. It continues to be an actively mined area. For much of the time that the Viburnum Trend has been mined, it has produced more lead annually than any other mining district in the world.

Southwest Missouri has also made a major contribution to the lead production in the state. This mining area, known as the Tri-State District, encompasses parts of Missouri, Kansas, and Oklahoma. Lead ore was mined near Oronogo, in Jasper County, as early as 1836. Large-scale mining began about 1851 in this part of the state. In 1870, large deposits of ore were discovered near Joplin. For nearly a century, the Tri-State District produced about 10 percent of the lead in the United States. However, the Tri-State District became most noted for its production of zinc. Zinc ore minerals and galena are frequently found in the same rocks. A small amount of lead has also been taken from six counties in central Missouri: Morgan, Miller, Camden, Moniteau, Cooper, and Cole. The amount of lead produced by this area has been rather small compared to the deposits in southeast Missouri.

Lead mining has had a major impact on Missouri's economy. The opening of new mines and processing facilities boosts local economies while another closing always means lost jobs and the accompanying economic problems. Many towns in the state owe their existence to the lead mining industry. Missouri continues to be the leading lead producer in the United States and was until very recently the leading producer in the world.

All production now comes from the Viburnum Trend. Numbers illustrate the significance of Missouri lead production. From 1988 to 1995, 73 to 90 percent of the lead produced in the United States came from Missouri. This represents a production of over two million tons of lead with a value of over two billion dollars. Missouri's mineral industry has even had an impact on the state's place names. In *Our Storehouse of Missouri Place Names,* Robert L. Ramsay states that there are more than twenty names related to Missouri's mineral wealth, including Galena in Stone County.

Lead produced from galena mined in Missouri is extremely pure (99.99 percent). This gives Missouri lead a distinct marketing advantage. Approximately 85 percent of Missouri's production is used in the manufacture of lead-acid batteries. The higher the purity of the lead used in making a battery, the more efficient its performance will be. In fact, for the manufacture of some special application batteries, Missouri lead is specified. Numerous electronic components also require very pure lead. Lead is also used in the glass for computer monitors and television screens.

In recognition of its leadership in the world as a lead-producing state, the Missouri legislature adopted galena as the official state mineral on July 21, 1967.

17

State Rock

Mozarkite

Chert is found in abundance in Missouri. Long before their first encounter with Europeans, Native Americans used chert for arrowheads and other items. An important industrial material today, chert occurs in most areas of the state in a wide array of colors. Because of its resistance to weathering, it has also affected the development of the landscape. A special variety of chert called mozarkite (named for the Missouri Ozarks) is especially colorful and distinctive in appearance. Mozarkite became the Missouri state rock on July 21, 1967.

Chert is composed of the mineral quartz, which is made up of silicon and oxygen (SiO_2), two of the most common elements on earth. Quartz sometimes forms crystals, but the quartz that makes up chert is in the form of microscopic grains.

The variety of colors in chert results from numerous impurities, such as iron, in the rock. These color variations give chert several names. Dark gray or black chert is usually called flint, and red chert is known as jasper. Chert made up of bands of color is called agate. Mozarkite is a particularly attractive form of chert, colored by various shades of red, pink, and purple with some green and gray tinting. According to Cheryl M. Seeger of the Missouri Geological Survey, any pink chert found in Missouri is considered to be mozarkite. Mozarkite is most commonly found in west-central Missouri, where it weathers out of the Cotter Dolomite. This formation dates back to the Ordovician period, which makes it about 450 mil-

Polished mozarkite is used for making jewelry.
(Missouri State Archives)

lion years old. Chert occurs both as layers, which may extend for long distances, and as individual round masses called nodules within limestone and dolomite.

Being made of quartz, chert is very resistant to weathering, while the carbonate minerals making up limestone and dolomite are easily eroded by slightly acidic water. This difference in weathering characteristics can affect how the landscape develops in areas where a substantial amount of chert occurs in the limestone. Layered chert can be left as overhanging ledges when surrounding carbonates are weathered away. This can lead to the formation of waterfalls such as Grand Falls on Shoal Creek near Joplin. High areas in the landscape can also result from the erosion of limestone and dolomite, which leaves the resistant chert. Chert accumulates as surface material in sizes ranging from boulders to gravel. This residual material is washed downhill by rainfall and is deposited in streambeds. For this reason, streambeds in the Ozarks are filled with chert gravel. It is moved and redeposited by the moving water, forming the familiar gravel bars in Missouri streams.

Archaeologists have found that Native Americans in what is now Missouri used chert before 10,000 B.C. It was readily available and relatively easy to fashion into points. Chert flakes off, when broken, leaving very sharp edges. Native Americans shaped chert in two ways. They used both the percussion method, in which one stone is struck with another, and pressure flaking, in which pressure is applied to the rock with a piece of bone or antler until a small chip breaks off. The process is continued until the point is completed. Indian sites are littered with many small pieces and flakes of chert left from these processes.

Modern inhabitants have continued to use chert for such things as a surface material on unpaved roads and as a mixing material in making concrete and asphalt for paved roads. Most chert is obtained from deposits where limestone has weathered away and left it exposed. In northern Missouri, there are also deposits of gravel of glacial origin. In southeastern Missouri, deposits of chert gravel made by streams during the Tertiary period, which began about sixty-five million years ago, are found on Crowley's Ridge.

Colorful forms of chert, such as mozarkite, can be polished. In fact, mozarkite is highly sought after nationwide for lapidary, the art of cutting and polishing stones to make jewelry.

The most common rock in the state, chert has multiple uses and has been used longer than any other mineral resource in the state. It is the foundation of the state's gravel industry with annual production in the millions of dollars. Many states have a rock symbol, but Missouri is the only state that has a rock whose name reflects the names of both the state itself and a particular region. With its beauty and usefulness, mozarkite serves well as the state rock.

18

State Fossil

Crinoid

While Missouri's recorded history has been long, its geologic history has been much longer. During the Precambrian period, over three billion years ago, lava from active volcanoes formed rocks on the surface while massive bodies of granite formed deep underground in what is now Missouri. These geologic events were followed by a period in which a barren landscape underwent extensive erosion. For millions of years shallow seas covered much of the state. Not all areas were covered at the same time, and some areas, such as the St. Francois Mountains in Iron and Madison Counties, were never submerged. Some areas eroded, while others received deposits.

The seas that covered the state contained abundant marine invertebrates, animals without backbones. These animals formed shells made of calcium carbonate and other material. Accumulated calcium carbonate from these shells led, in part, to the formation of large deposits of limestone within the state. Occasionally, remains of these marine animals have been so well preserved in the limestone that paleontologists can determine a great deal about their size and in what conditions they lived.

These remains, referred to as fossils, could be formed in several ways. The organism might have left an impression in soft sediments, or the hard parts of the animal might have been preserved or replaced by other minerals. Missouri has

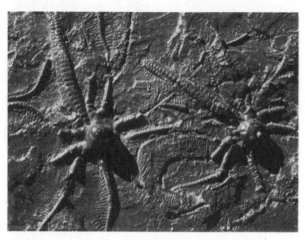

Crinoids were abundant in the seas covering parts of Missouri during the Mississippian and Pennsylvanian periods. (Missouri State Archives)

many rock formations that are rich in fossils. They provide information about the organisms that lived in the distant past, and they serve as a correlation between two different rock formations. That is to say, the same fossil found in two different locations indicates to geologists that the rocks were formed at the same time. They also help determine the conditions under which the rocks containing the fossils were formed.

On June 16, 1989, the crinoid was adopted as Missouri's state fossil after a group of students from Lee's Summit School promoted the idea. Crinoids were some of the first fossils that humans recognized. They belong to the phylum Echinoderma. Living members of this phylum include starfish, sea urchins, and sand dollars. Modern examples of crinoids are sea lilies and feather stars. Today, crinoids are found primarily in the Indian and Pacific Oceans and in the Caribbean Sea.

Most fossil crinoids were animals that lived attached to the seafloor. They consisted of a cup, or calyx, which housed the organism's soft parts and organs. Arms extended out and up from the cup to gather food. A stem consisting of a series of plates extended downward to a rootlike structure that anchored the crinoid to the sea floor. Crinoids first appear in the fossil record during the Ordovician period, which began about 495 million years ago. During the Mississippian period, about 360 million years ago, there was an explosion in the population and development of crinoids. In later geologic periods, their numbers dramatically decreased. At their peak, during the Mississippian and Pennsylvanian periods, crinoids occurred in such numbers that some areas of the seafloor would have been a "garden" of crinoids.

Crinoid fossils are abundant in Missouri rocks. In fact, some of the best-known crinoid-bearing formations in North America are found in Missouri. The Burlington Formation, formed during the Mississippian period, contains some beds composed almost entirely of crinoid remains. Rocks formed during the Pennsylvanian period in the Kansas City area have yielded the best crinoid fossils of that age, including *Delocrinus missouriensis,* the crinoid that has been designated the state fossil.

While the remains of a creature that lived millions of years ago may not seem like a very exciting symbol, the crinoid reminds us of the processes and the millions of years required to form the landscape of Missouri.

19

Missouri Day

Missouri has one symbol unlike all of the others. It is not an object but a day: Missouri Day was established in 1915 to recognize Missouri people, places, and historical events. It offers an opportunity to draw attention to the state and promote Missouri products and tourism.

In 1909, Anna Brosius Korn, a native of Caldwell County, was living in El Reno, Oklahoma. She became a charter member and officer of the Missouri Society of Oklahoma that year. Such organizations were not uncommon in those days and served to bring together native Missourians living in an adoptive state. This experience and her love for her native state led Korn to believe that there was a need to unite all of the various organizations relating to Missouri and give them a common focus. In Korn's words, it would be "a day when Missourians at home and abroad could meet and observe universally." Korn even wrote a song about her beloved state, which was considered as a possible state song by Missouri's legislature in 1913.

After moving to Trenton, Missouri, a short time later, Korn devoted her full efforts to the establishment of a day named for the state. In 1913, she drafted a resolution for Missouri Day to be observed October 1. Supporters introduced her resolution at meetings of a variety of statewide organizations, such as Missouri Daughters of the American Revolution, State Teachers Association, Missouri Bankers Association, and

Missouri United Daughters of the Confederacy, all of which accepted it.

With the support of so many organizations, Korn drafted a bill, which J. A. Waterman, representative from Caldwell County, introduced on January 11, 1915. During committee hearings, the date was changed from October 1 to the first Monday in October. The bill passed the house January 26 and the senate March 19, 1915, and was signed by Governor Elliott Major March 22, 1915. In 1969, the observance of Missouri Day was moved from the first Monday to the third Wednesday in October.

Missouri Day is not a holiday in the traditional sense; businesses are not closed. It is a way to encourage schools to focus on Missouri and Missouri history. The day also provides an opportunity for Missourians to learn more about their state, to promote Missouri and its products, and for the people of the state to celebrate the achievements of all Missourians.

20

Missouri's Nickname

All fifty states have nicknames, many derived from plants or animals identified with the states. For example, Maine is known as the Pine Tree State and Michigan as the Wolverine State. Other nicknames stem from natural features present within a state. Arizona is known as the Grand Canyon State. Some nicknames derive from historical attitudes of the residents—Tennessee is know as the Volunteer State. Missouri's nickname, the Show-Me State, captures the essence of its people's character.

The general assembly has never enacted legislation officially designating a state nickname, although numerous nicknames have been associated with the state during its history. Because of its role in the lead industry, it is sometimes called the "Lead State." Missouri is also known as the "Cave State" due to the large number of caves within its borders. Data from the Missouri Division of Geology and Land Survey shows fifty-one hundred caves in the state. Other nicknames include "Bullion State," from Senator Thomas Hart Benton's insistence on a monetary standard based on gold and silver, and "Mule Capital of the World" because of Missouri's prominence in the mule trade. Missouri also became known as the "Outlaw State" immediately after the Civil War, when lawless gangs like that of the James brothers were so prevalent.

The nickname that has become almost universally associated with Missouri is the "Show-Me State." This nickname is probably better known than the official state motto, "Let the welfare of the people be the supreme law," which is on the state seal. The "Show-Me" nickname now appears on letterheads and license plates in Missouri. It is used in association with state government programs and the promotion of products and tourism. It appears in the names of athletic events and businesses. It has even been used to name public buildings. The Show-Me Center, a large multipurpose building on the campus of Southeast Missouri State University, is an example.

Several explanations of the origin of this nickname have been offered. The most widespread credits Willard Vandiver, congressman from Missouri's fourteenth district from 1896 to 1902, with the phrase "I am from Missouri. You have got to show me." Vandiver reportedly used the phrase in an 1899 speech before the Five O'Clock Club in Philadelphia when the Congressional Naval Affairs Committee was visiting that city to consider expansion of shipyards there.

Recent research by Barry Popik, an attorney and slang historian in New York, and Gerald Cohen, a professor at the University of Missouri–Rolla, has shown this explanation to be in error. Vandiver's speech was not given until January 27, 1900, and Popik and Cohen have found irrefutable evidence that the Kansas City delegation to the 1898 Trans-Mississippi Exposition held in Omaha, Nebraska, employed the expression as its slogan. The exposition highlighted development and economic and community growth in all areas west of the Mississippi River. The display lasted four months and covered 108 city blocks.

Cohen and Popik discovered that newspapers of the time in both Omaha and Kansas City frequently referred to the expression, "I'm from Missouri, you've got to show me." A group of more than one thousand Kansas City residents traveled to Omaha in August 1898. Both the *Kansas City Star* and *Omaha Daily Bee* reported that these visitors had the "show-me" slogan inscribed on their badges. Vandiver simply adopted the expression, which was already well known and widely used. In fact, contemporary newspaper accounts of the dinner where Vandiver spoke make only slight mention of his speech. Popik and Cohen's research shows that only a 1911 article in the *New York Herald* credits Vandiver as originator of the nickname.

The phrase has come to be associated with the attitude often exhibited by Missouri's citizens, individuals who are practical and who carefully assess new ideas and approaches before accepting them. They tend to expect proof, rather than opinions or speculation. The nickname has also come to stand for the eagerness of natives to show Missouri's accomplishments and its attractions to visitors. Most Missourians would probably say, "If there is a better nickname than the one we have, you'll have to show me!"

21

How Laws Are Made

State symbols are made official through the legislative process that produces all the state's laws. The process begins when a legislator, an individual, or a group has an idea for a law or a symbol. For example, the idea for naming the honeybee as the state insect originated with the Missouri State Beekeepers Association. Once the idea exists, the individual or group interested in specific legislation drafts a bill. A legislator or legislative staff may then write the actual bill.

Once a bill has been written, it is filed by a legislator with the clerk of the house or the senate. Bills may be introduced in either the house of representatives or the senate, but all appropriation bills originate in the house. Once filed, the bill is read to introduce it. This is called the *first reading*. The bill is then ordered to be printed and goes to its *second reading*. Following the second reading, it is assigned to a committee for review. This assignment is made in the house by the speaker of the house and in the senate by the president of the senate.

The committee holds hearings on the bill and makes a recommendation. If the committee makes a favorable report, the bill is then debated on the floor of the house and that of the senate, and sometimes amendments are offered. A vote is taken. If approved, the bill is said to be *perfected*. It is then printed again and scheduled for a third reading and final vote. If it is approved in the final vote, the bill is then sent to the other house of the general assembly, where it undergoes a similar process. If the house and senate pass different versions of the bill, then a *conference committee* composed of members from both houses meets to work out a compromise. When both houses pass the same bill, the bill is said to be *truly agreed to and finally passed.*

The measure is then sent to the governor, who can either sign it, veto it, or do nothing. If the governor signs, the bill it is sent to the secretary of state to be included in the state laws. If he vetoes the bill, it is returned to its house of origin. If the governor does not act on a bill within the time specified in the state constitution, it becomes law just as if the governor had signed it.

22

A Proposed Symbol and a New Symbol

The list of state symbols will never really be complete. From time to time, various groups propose new symbols. Their purpose may be to promote one of the state's products or to simply highlight some aspect of Missouri's heritage. As this manuscript was being prepared for publication, two new symbols were under consideration by the general assembly. In the spring of 2003, bills naming big bluestem as the state grass and Norton/Cynthiana as the state grape were meandering their way through the legislative process.

The idea for big bluestem as the state grass originated with Chris Schmidgall's fourth grade class at Truman Elementary School in Rolla during the class's study of prairie ecosystems. When Representative Bob May spoke to the class about state government, they, in Schmidgall's words, "connected the dots" and presented their idea for a new state symbol to him. Representative May and Senator Sarah Steelman then assisted the students in getting a bill written. The two legislators introduced the measure in their respective houses of the legislature. The class chose four of its members to appear before house and senate committees reviewing the bill, which won approval in the house but didn't come to a vote in the senate.

Prior to settlement, prairie covered most of western Missouri and practically all of the state north of the Missouri River. Grass dominates the vegetation of prairies. Although trees

On July 11, 2003, Governor Bob Holden signed a bill making the Norton/Cynthiana Missouri's state grape. (Drawing of Norton from *The Grapes of New York*, 1907, courtesy Western Historical Manuscript Collection, Columbia)

occur within the prairie landscape, they do not form large continuous tracts of forest. Of the several species of grasses covering the presettlement prairie of Missouri, big bluestem (*Andropogon geradii*) was one of the most abundant.

The Missouri Grape and Wine Advisory Board along with the Missouri Grape Growers Association proposed a state grape to help promote the state's growing grape and wine industry. The bill, introduced in the senate by Sarah Steelman, received approval there. The house passed the measure on April 24, 2003, and it was delivered to the governor.

The variety chosen for this distinction, the Norton/ Cynthiana (*Vitis aestivalis*), a native American grape, first came to the attention of growers in Virginia in the 1830s, who referred to it as Norton's Virginia. It was planted in the Hermann area in the 1840s by a number of growers, including George Husmann, who later became a professor at the University of Missouri. According to Husmann, the Norton revolutionized grape culture in Missouri, leading to national and international awards for Missouri wines. In the 1850s, plant breeders found a similar grape growing in Arkansas called Cynthiana. Husmann's biographer, Linda Walker Stevens, writes that he received Cynthiana from New York in 1858. He worked with cuttings from these vines and found that their grapes produced outstanding wine as well. These two grapes became the foundation of Missouri's wine industry until Prohibition ended commercial wine production in Missouri. Because of their similarities, horticulturists debated whether Norton and Cynthiana represented one or two varieties.

The debate continues today. Genetic tests conducted by several universities reveal no differences between them, thus the combined name. Norton/Cynthiana, disease-resistant and well adapted to the state's climate, plays a major role in Missouri's growing wine industry. Wines made from these grapes finish well up in the rankings in competitions.

Appendix

Chronological List of State Symbols

State Seal	1822
State Flag	1913
Missouri Day	1915
Present Capitol Building completed	1917
State Flower, Hawthorn	1923
State Bird, Bluebird	1927
State Song, "Missouri Waltz"	1949
State Tree, Dogwood	1955
State Mineral, Galena	1967
State Rock, Mozarkite	1967
State Insect, Honeybee	1985
State Musical Instrument, Fiddle	1987
State Fossil, Crinoid	1989
State Tree Nut, Black Walnut	1990
State American Folk Dance, Square Dance	1995
State Animal, Mule	1995
State Aquatic Animal, Paddlefish	1997
State Fish, Channel Catfish	1997
State Horse, Missouri Fox Trotting Horse	2002
State Grape, Norton/Cynthiana	2003

For More Reading

Bees and Beekeeping, by Roger A. Morse (Ithaca, N.Y.: Cornell University Press, 1975), describes the honeybee and covers all aspects of beekeeping.

The Common Fossils of Missouri, by A. G. Unklesbay (Columbia: University of Missouri Press, 1955), discusses those fossils most likely to be encountered in Missouri.

"Dogwoods for American Gardens," a University of Tennessee Extension publication, may be found at the website, *www.utextension.utk.edu/pbfiles/PB1670.pdf.* This publication discusses the origin of the name "dogwood" and provides detailed information about growing and caring for varieties of dogwood trees.

"Early Horseback Riding in Steppes—Summary," on the Hartwick College Institute for Ancient Equestrian Studies website, *http://users.hartwick.edu/iaes/horseback/summary.html,* summarizes the institute's research on the wear on teeth of ancient horses and its relationship to the development of horseback riding. There is also much other information about man's early use of the horse.

The Fiddle Book, by Marion Thede (New York: Oak Publications, 1967), provides a history of the instrument and its music and discusses playing techniques.

A Field Guide to the Birds, by Roger Tory Peterson (Boston: Houghton Mifflin, 1947), discusses identification and habits of birds.

The Fishes of Missouri, by William L. Pflieger (Jefferson City: Missouri Department of Conservation, 1988), furnishes detailed information about native fish, including channel catfish and paddlefish.

Forum Anglicum: Studies in Slang 6, by Gerald Cohen and Barry Popik (Frankfort: Peter Lang, 1999), offers detailed research into the origin of Missouri's nickname.

Hammons Products, Stockton, Missouri, website, *www.black_ walnut.com,* contains extensive information about the production and use of black walnut products.

The History of Missouri Capitols, by Marian M. Ohman (Columbia: University of Missouri, Extension Division, 1982), is a great book, discussing the location and building of all of Missouri's capitols.

"History of the MFTHBA," on the Missouri Fox Trotting Horse Breed Association website, *http://www.mfthba.com/The MFTHBAAAssoc.html,* has a history of the breed and information about registry and the organization's calendar of activities.

"Legacy of the Horse," on the International Museum of the Horse website, *http://www.imh.org/imh/exh1.html,* provides detailed information about the origins and uses of various breeds.

Missouri Geology, by A. G. Unklesbay and Jerry D. Vineyard (Columbia: University of Missouri Press, 1973), is an excellent reference on the state's geology.

Missouri: The Heart of the Nation, second edition by William E. Parrish, Charles T. Jones, Jr., and Lawrence O. Christensen (Arlington Heights, Ill.: Harlan Davidson, 1992), is an excellent general history.

The Missouri Mule: His Origin and Times, two volumes, by Melvin Bradley (Columbia: University of Missouri, Extension Division, 1993), is a comprehensive book on the origins, characteristics, and uses of the mule by the leading authority on the subject.

Missouri Old-Time Fiddling website, *www.missourifiddling.com*, features articles on Missouri fiddle traditions and links to contests.

Missouri Trees, by J. E. Wylie and Ramon Gass (Jefferson City: Missouri Department of Conservation, 1980), provides a description of native trees.

Only the Rivers Are Peaceful: Thomas Hart Benton's Missouri Mural, by Bob Priddy (Independence: Herald Publishing, 1989), provides a detailed discussion of the paintings in the capitol building.

A Peterson Field Guide to Medicinal Plants, Eastern and Central North America, by Steven Foster and James A. Duke (Boston: Houghton Mifflin, 1990) discusses native plants, including black walnut and hawthorn, and their medicinal uses.

The Prehistory of Missouri, by Michael J. O'Brien and W. Raymond Wood (Columbia: University of Missouri Press, 1998), furnishes information about the state's first inhabitants, including their use of chert in toolmaking.

A Time to Dance: American Country Dancing from Hornpipes to Hot Hash, by Richard Nevell (New York: St. Martin's Press, 1977), traces the history of American folk dance. It features photographs, line drawings, and old wood engravings of dance steps.

Trees for Urban Missouri, by James P. Rocca, Dale Starkey, and Eldon Heflin (Jefferson City: Missouri Department of Conservation, 1979), describes trees suitable for urban landscapes.

Turbulent Partnership: Missouri and the Union, 1861-1865, by William E. Parrish (Columbia: University of Missouri Press, 1963), focuses on the tensions in Missouri during the Civil War.

Index

About the Author

John C. Fisher, a freelance writer, lives in
Kennett, Missouri.